THE PATH TO THE PINNACLE

ADVANCE PRAISE

"The Pinnacle approach changes the way you view and operate your business on a daily basis. It helps you to build a foundation of A players that live your CORE values, create winning playbooks, and drive clarity and alignment around your purpose and goals. Our performance metrics and goals have increased at every level throughout the organization, and our entire team now understands the why. If I could change one thing, I would have started working with Pinnacle earlier."

—BRANDON MENSINK, COO & CO-OWNER
OF TONNA MECHANICAL, INC.

"Greg and Michael's experience and knowledge in helping companies maximize their performance and achieve newfound levels of success is both extensive and impressive. The Pinnacle system's track record of success is simply too good to ignore, and The Path to the Pinnacle is a must-read for any business owner or entrepreneur. I'm grateful for their guidance, and you will be too."

—CHRIS MAXSON, OWNER & CEO OF ACUCRAFT FIREPLACES

"*I am grateful for all that you and Pinnacle have done for Vision Management. I remember the day you introduced me to Pinnacle, and I am so pleased with the decision to move to Pinnacle. In my humble opinion, nothing compares to Pinnacle, you, or your guides. You all are such talented and valuable assets. The attention you give to our business, our rocks, plans, growth, and the personal interaction are second to none. Our explosive growth, reputation in the market, and profitability are all due to Pinnacle and the processes. Thank you for all you do for Vision, my team, and myself. It is greatly appreciated!*"

—TONY FIORILLO, CEO OF VISION MANAGEMENT GROUP

"'*What worked then doesn't work now.' No words have been truer to business leaders that have been part of growing a company. The speed at which we are having to adapt as leaders is unprecedented. Having an operating system that is best in class, flexible, and built for growth like Pinnacle gives us the framework to evolve the system as the business evolves. Greg and Michael have created a tremendous system designed to move you through every phase of business.*"

—EMILY MORGAN, FOUNDER & CEO OF DELEGATE SOLUTIONS AND AUTHOR OF *LET IT GO!*

"*Greg and Michael have put together a great package! The facts, statistics, analogies, and experts Greg and Michael bring to life in this book and in their actual practice provide a roadmap to success! Thanks, Greg and Michael. I will meet you at the top!*"

—GARY M RYCHLEY 任雷, PRESIDENT OF FASTEST INC.

"*The Pinnacle approach is customizable, nimble, and applicable to any business challenge. It layers the latest business thinking on top of tried-and-true practices. This unique combination continues to take my company and leadership to the next level."*

—KRISTI PIEHL, FOUNDER & CEO OF MEDIA MINEFIELD

"As an executive in a Fortune 100 organization leading three different operating lines of business, I've been using foundational Business Operating Systems for years. When I first encountered Next Level Growth, I was excited to see the agility and adaptability of the system. Having a flexible and comprehensive system allows for flexibility and evolution as the business grows to nine-figures and beyond, and it allows me to be a more streamlined and effective leader."

—RAJIV PATEL, MD, MBA, FACP, PRESIDENT OF HEALTH CARE ENTERPRISES PROVIDER STRATEGY AT CENTENE CORPORATION

"In our early days, we struggled with the limitations of our EOS Implementer, and the restrictiveness of the system impeded our growth in many ways. When we transitioned to Next Level Growth, we found that their approach and guidance was tailored to us, and focused on us, over purity to a prescriptive system. The additional tools and concepts we learned, and the way we were encouraged to challenge our way of thinking, has led to significant breakthroughs that have us now disrupting our industry.

We've been listed on the Inc. 5000 list the last three years in a row. That doesn't happen by accident. That happens when a leadership team is focused and intentional about what they do on a daily basis. Thanks to our work with Next Level Growth, we are growing into a sustainable business that transcends the founders and is moving to become a global source for good."

—RYAN WOODWARD, PRESIDENT & CEO OF NATIONAL TECHNICAL INSTITUTE

"*Everything we do focuses on the whole process—having the right people, the right coaching, the right purposes, and the right operations—which the Pinnacle model is built on. Because we share the same values, we fit in very well with the Pinnacle Guides and their approach to help businesses grow. There's a shared sense of purpose because we're on the journey together.*"

—JODY GRUNDEN, CPA, PARTNER AT SUMMIT CPA

"*Greg and Michael are the rarest of the rare. Their skill and understanding of business is only matched by their generosity in sharing that knowledge. The Path to the Pinnacle is so full of insights that the only reason I wanted to put it down was to run and start putting those nuggets to use! The Pinnacle Business Operating System, and the community that supports it, is revolutionizing the world of Business Operating Systems. With the work they and so many others have done, it's clear that they've cemented themselves as the 'Category of 1' in Business Operating Systems. This book serves as the exclamation point on that achievement. Congratulations!*"

—KYLE MEALY, VICE PRESIDENT OF
GROWTH AT ROCKET CLICKS

"*The Next Level Growth approach has given our company the confidence it needs to work through tough strategic issues, make decisions, and set ourselves up for exponential growth, not just growth for growth's sake. We are now focused on sustainable, purpose-driven growth that will make a huge impact for our employees and our community. If you're looking for a system to provide the tools you need to organize your business and reach your goals, then reading this book is a great start. I can't say enough about the impact Next Level Growth has made on our business.*"

—SCOTT LEHMAN, FOUNDER AND VISIONARY
AT PREMIER AUTO CENT

"Working with Greg and Michael has been transformative. The Pinnacle Operating System has increased our focus, accountability, communication, and transparency. Our Leadership Team utilizes the tools to advance our company in every way—Vision, Purpose, People, and Process. We have just begun our climb to the top, but working with the Pinnacle system will be integral to our success."

—JOHN DEMPSEY, PRESIDENT OF DEMPSEY CONSTRUCTION

"In addition to his own unique proven processes and the customizable approach he brings to the table, Michael is a true leader who has been there and knows how to best engage and lead. His ability to read people and situations to flush out real issues has brought clarity and accountability to the forefront of our time together. It's been transformational in every sense. Michael has been instrumental in constantly sharpening our highly functional team and is a big part of our continued success!"

—JEFF CHANDLER, CEO & PRESIDENT OF HIBAR
HOSPITALITY GROUP AND HOPDODDY BURGER BAR

"Greg encourages our leadership team to celebrate successes. He also challenges us by asking the important (sometimes uncomfortable) questions combined with practical advice in moving forward together. Greg is continually adapting, learning, and growing his skills and tools to enable his clients on their own unique paths of continual improvement."

—STEFAN FREEMAN, PRESIDENT & CEO OF BANKVISTA

"Running a business successfully is great, but it is different from growing a business successfully. So if your vision is to keep evolving and scaling, you need a system and set of tools that will evolve and scale with you. Evolving systems and strategies are necessary to successfully reach higher and higher levels.

Working with Next Level Growth has given us the visibility, humility, and resources we've needed to maintain our velocity at every stage of our entrepreneurial journey."

—J.P. DAHDAH, FOUNDER & CEO OF
VANTAGE RETIREMENT PLANS, LLC

"Michael is an incredible leader, mentor, and coach. He has helped level up Upward Projects, as well as my own professional growth. If you are looking to grow your company, Next Level Growth is a must."

—BRENT RENNER, CHIEF DEVELOPMENT OFFICER
AT UPWARD PROJECTS RESTAURANT GROUP

"When our parents retired, my brother Michael and I continued to manage the business the same way, as a mom-and-pop business, and we quickly hit a ceiling that lasted many years. Self-implementing operating systems like 4DX and EOS helped us break through those initial ceilings, but it was bringing in the guidance of Michael Erath and his unique approach that truly accelerated our growth. We will hit our BHAG in 2023, several years ahead of schedule! Most importantly, working with Michael and Next Level Growth has helped us to create a business that gives us freedom rather than ties us down."

—RYAN KALMBACH, OWNER & VISIONARY AT
JOHNSTONE SUPPLY, THE ORION GROUP

"Greg has been an invaluable asset to the growth of our business over the past six years. His vast business experience and intuitive thinking has given us a leap forward that would have otherwise been unattainable. Pinnacle is a must for any business looking to grow and be competitive in today's high-tech environment."

—DAVID & JONATHAN DWORSKY, PARK CHRYSLER JEEP

"After leveling up our operating system and moving beyond EOS, our team has a much clearer picture of where we are going, how each of them contribute to our vision, and how their success is measured. In just three years, we were able to double revenue and quadruple profit, all while focusing our time and effort on the areas we wanted to, instead of firefighting all day, every day.

In 2022, we were able to reach our BHAG and exit the company, leaving the team on solid footing for continued growth well into the future."

—CHRIS PRENOVOST, STRATEGIST AT AZPRO

"Greg Cleary has worked with our organization for the past five years, helping guide us through the implementation of our first Business Operating System. Greg's creative approach utilizes an effective mix of strategic thinking, goal setting, tools, metrics, and constant feedback, which has helped propel our team forward."

—BO GEBBIE, PRESIDENT OF EVOLVING SOLUTIONS, INC.

"Four years after leaving EOS, we're still working with Greg and Pinnacle because of the value he continues to bring with his insight, knowledge, and tools."

—KEVIN KOPPANG, GENERAL MANAGER AT
COMSTOCK CONSTRUCTION, INC.

"Greg is the real deal. He has a God-given ability to instantly pierce through all of our ego and noise to see the pieces of gold we already possess and the coal that needs refining. Beyond that, he has an uncanny ability to lead people to the answers they're looking for. He's truly one of a kind and an irreplaceable asset to anyone who seeks his guidance."

—RICK SAND, ATTORNEY AT SAND LAW, PLLC

THE PATH TO THE PINNACLE

USING CUSTOMIZED BUSINESS OPERATING SYSTEMS TO DRIVE GROWTH

GREGORY CLEARY ◬ MICHAEL ERATH

LIONCREST
PUBLISHING

COPYRIGHT © 2023 GREGORY CLEARY & MICHAEL ERATH

THE PATH TO THE PINNACLE
Using Customized Business Operating Systems to Drive Growth

FIRST EDITION

ISBN   978-1-5445-4236-2 *Hardcover*
       978-1-5445-4235-5 *Paperback*
       978-1-5445-4234-8 *Ebook*

CONTENTS

INTRODUCTION

ONE SIZE DOES NOT FIT ALL

"What's dangerous is not to evolve."

—JEFF BEZOS

"One-size-fits-all means it doesn't fit anybody."

—SAMANTHA CLEARY (AT FIFTEEN YEARS OLD)

There's a problem in the world of Business Operating Systems: they're not evolving. Many of them have been using the same tools and the same approach for decades, but if experience has taught us anything, it's that there's always a better way. An approach that worked for you ten years ago, or five years ago, or last year might not work for you today. Some new tool, concept, or approach that you just discovered might be better than what you've been doing.

If you're not ready and willing to embrace better methods, tools, and concepts, then you may struggle to surmount the obstacles of tomorrow. To that end, we've always encouraged the guides at Pinnacle to seek, learn, evolve, and grow. After all, that is the very essence of visionary leadership! While we believe in establishing best practices and having a set of tools that you can use as a starting point, we are also strong believers in using a freestyle approach with the companies who rope us in to help guide them to the summits of their business mountains.

If something isn't working for them, we go into our tool shed or out into our network of thought leaders and find another tool that will work and bring it back. That's how we do things at Pinnacle today, but it wasn't always that way. Before we founded Pinnacle, we used to live in the world of the "one-size-fits-all" approach of Business Operating Systems. But we found ourselves constantly at odds with that approach and always felt like we had to take a more freestyle approach to get the best results for our clients.

Individuals inherently desire to exert influence over the trajectory of their lives. Allow us to share a poignant story from one of our guides that resonates deeply with us.

Julie, the wife of one of our guides, was confronted with a breast cancer diagnosis. This news, coupled with the responsibility of caring for two young children, engendered an overwhelming sense of stress and realization regarding the far-reaching implications of breast cancer. It is important to note that this occurred two decades ago, when receiving a breast cancer diagnosis often signified a life-altering event.

Julie was referred to a renowned university hospital in her city, where she was informed that chemotherapy was the sole treatment modality available for her particular type of breast cancer. However, Julie harbored reservations regarding chemotherapy. She pondered how her children would react to her hair loss and apprehended the impact of enduring weeks of chemotherapy, taking into account the tales she had heard about its pervasive effects on daily life.

Seeking a second opinion, Julie embarked on extensive research and found herself directed to another oncologist who specifically specialized in breast cancer and had overwhelmingly positive reviews from patients. All her medical files and test results were forwarded to this physician. Julie had heard that this doctor was renowned for adopting a patient-centric approach, considering the individual as a whole during the course of treatment.

Within moments of meeting the oncologist, it became evident that his playbook or approach differed markedly. He gazed directly into Julie's eyes and assured her, "Julie, you will conquer this cancer. It is highly treatable, and you will survive." Overwhelmed with relief, Julie was moved to tears. She had discovered someone willing to listen and provide reassurance that she would overcome this ordeal.

The doctor engaged in a heartfelt conversation with Julie, attentively learning about her unique circumstances and concerns. He recognized the fear reflected in her eyes, particularly regarding the impact on her children and the potential ramifications of not being there for them in the long term. Julie candidly expressed her reservations regarding chemotherapy. Following what felt like an hour-long dialogue, the doctor presented a treatment protocol based on Julie's feedback:

1. Immediate surgery aimed at removing 95 percent of the cancer, assuming it had not metastasized.
2. Post-surgery, a course of seven rounds of radiation therapy to ensure eradication of any residual tissue.
3. Regular follow-ups and monitoring through blood work. Chemotherapy remained a viable option, to be considered if the first two approaches did not yield the desired outcomes.

Fast forward two decades, and we are delighted to share that Julie is thriving, free from cancer, while her two children are excelling and pursuing their education in college.

This anecdote underscores a fundamental truth: a single approach does not suit all circumstances. Individuals possess unique needs and preferences. Some may elect to follow the recommendations of a prestigious university hospital, while others seek the autonomy to make choices and actively participate in their own journeys. Pinnacle, at its core, embraces the concept of involving you in the path you undertake to foster the growth of your business.

Choose your guide, let them inside the business, and have rich conversations. Use the guides experience to build a plan that you are all-in on executing and are excited about. The guide in many ways is more important than the tools in their toolbox. It's how they apply those tools and in what order that really makes the difference.

At Pinnacle, instead of following a predetermined process that applies the same to every client regardless of their situation, we meet clients where they are. We set an agenda based on their objectives and find the right path and the right pace for their unique situation and goals.

DRAWING OUTSIDE THE LINES

With a wealth of experience as highly successful coaches in the realm of Business Operating Systems, Gregory and Michael have established a strong track record. Gregory Cleary, in particular, has dedicated his entire professional life to coaching, beginning with his involvement in esteemed organizations such as Brian Tracy Learning Systems, Peak Performers Network, and Team Trac. In 2001, he took a significant step forward by founding his own coaching company, Action Learning, which focused on delivering training in leadership, sales, and customer service.

Driven by a relentless pursuit of expanding his expertise, Gregory traveled to Detroit in 2010 to acquire a certification as an EOS Implementer. Joining in its early stages, he consistently demonstrated remarkable growth, earning well-deserved recognition for his invaluable contributions throughout the years. In 2018, Gregory attended his first Scaling Up Summit, and in the fall of 2019, he pursued a certification with Scaling Up to further enhance his coaching credentials. It was in March 2020 when Gregory, along with Duane Marshall, a trusted coach and close friend of Michael's, launched Pinnacle.

Drawing from his extensive experience in the training business, Gregory recognized that no single individual possesses an exclusive monopoly on good ideas. Therefore, he made it his mission to curate the finest tools available, which could be shared with his clients to facilitate their growth and success.

As recounted in his book *RISE: The Reincarnation of an Entrepreneur*, published in 2017, Michael Erath came to the world of Business Operating Systems by a different path, but he wound up in a similar place. He spent more than twenty years owning and building multiple businesses in the hardwood timber industry, and during that time, he studied several different approaches and thought leaders in the world of Business Operating Systems. As a voracious reader of business books, Michael began implementing many different tools and concepts that he had read about in order to improve his businesses.

Eventually, a colleague of his, and fellow EO member from Columbus, Ohio, asked him if he would help his executive team implement a Business Operating System, since Michael had been successful with the system he implemented in his own business. Michael agreed, and during that process, he realized he had a real passion and gift for using his own experience and background to help other business leaders. As a result, he eventually exited his businesses and became a full time Business Guide in May of 2015.

As Michael's success as a Business Guide accelerated, he soon crossed paths with Gregory Cleary, who was also working with and teaching the same Business Operating System. They would often sit together during quarterly meetings, and both expressed a similar vision for stepping outside the lines of the purity of Business Operating Systems.

Gregory became a mentor to Michael, and more importantly, a good friend. As their vision for a more customizable, outcomes-based approach began to become clear, they eventually wound up leaving the system they were working in and joining forces.

They worked together to develop a radically different approach, a customizable framework that enables visionary leaders to leverage a wide variety of tools and tactics, regardless of the source, to create systems that work best for them, in their unique circumstances.

They weren't simply creating a new system and crossing their fingers that clients would like it. They already knew that business leaders were clamoring for a customizable system. Gregory had created a Mastermind group for the top twenty-five coaches from the system they were part of at the time. That group met quarterly, and from discussions that arose within the Mastermind group, it became clear that many of their clients craved this new, customizable approach.

That peer group proved to be a powerful force for evolutionary change. They would often create new tools, bring them to the group, and share how they were evolving to meet client needs. The peer group provided feedback and helped them refine their approach.

In fact, this peer group formed the core of what became Pinnacle. Most of them became the founding members of the organization—the very first Pinnacle Business Guides. Soon, Pinnacle was a fast-growing coaching organization, and at the time of this writing, it is closing in on 150 Business Guides. Pinnacle could grow even faster, but Gregory, Michael, and Duane have set a very high bar for excellence and turn away many applicants for membership simply because they lack the experience to be the best of the best.

THE PINNACLE OF BUSINESS OPERATING SYSTEMS

So, what *are* people looking for? What is this new approach? This thing called "The Pinnacle of Business Operating Systems"?

With a one-size-fits-all approach, you have a series of nonnegotiable steps that all clients are required to take. Everything must be implemented the same way with every client. That means following the same onboarding path regardless of the organization's unique circumstances and maintaining the same meeting structure regardless of the unique needs of the moment.

Pinnacle is a comprehensive Business Operating System designed to facilitate the growth of businesses. We often use the metaphor of climbing a mountain to illustrate the process. It is important to note that smaller, more cohesive leadership teams can progress up the mountain more efficiently compared to larger teams that lack alignment and commitment to the company's direction.

Rather than adopting a one-size-fits-all approach, we dedicate two to three days to assess the company's and team's overall health. This intensive session, similar to a three-day annual check-up at the Mayo Clinic, involves a thorough examination of your current situation. By the time you leave Base Camp, you will have a Strategic Vision and Execution Plan that identifies the obstacles hindering your progress and highlights the areas requiring focus for achieving "Profitable Growth." Our Base Camp sessions combine the best of both worlds: a structured framework and the expertise of experienced guides, enabling you to prioritize effectively and achieve quick victories.

At the conclusion of Base Camp, your team will emerge as a

united front, armed with precise steps to propel the company forward before the next Summit with your Guide.

Our Quarterly Summits are entirely client-driven and centered around three key objectives:

1. Look Back: Evaluate progress and celebrate accomplishments.
2. Look Out: Establish the FAST Rocks in alignment with the Annual Growth Plan for the upcoming ninety days.
3. Look Up: Think bigger and aim higher. The Guide challenges you to confront difficult topics and make bold decisions that promote growth.

What sets Pinnacle apart is the vast toolbox at our disposal, consisting of over eighty tools that Guides can select from for each Summit with your team. While there are seven Bedrock Tools that every leadership team must master, we constantly strive to deliver the right tool at the right time. Our toolbox remains open-ended and continuously evolving, always focused on delivering the highest gains in the shortest possible timeframe.

Ultimately, our goal is to provide you with a CUSTOMIZED and PERSONALIZED Business Operating System that evolves alongside your organization. Your leadership team even has the opportunity to name various components, such as Daily Stand-Ups and Weekly Tactical meetings, ensuring their relevance and engagement.

By leveraging Pinnacle, you have the flexibility to retain and optimize the elements of your existing Business Operating

System that are effective, while upgrading and enhancing those that require improvement.

As it has evolved, the essence of our approach comes down to a simple formula that can be customized for every business situation:

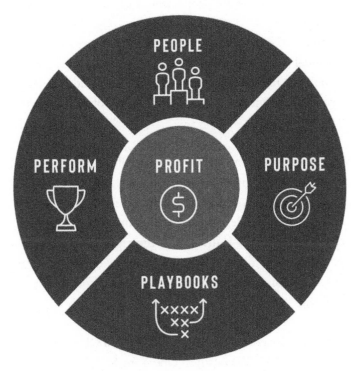

People + Purpose + Playbooks + Perform = Profit

As we tell our leadership teams, growing your business always starts with great **people**. If you want to 5X your business, you must 5X your people. To put it another way, before you set out to summit a mountain, you need to make sure you have the right people on the team to climb with you. You also must make sure your team members possess the right blend of skillsets to meet your needs on the climb. And you must make sure everyone is prepared and knows the path ahead.

Once you have the right people, you need to make sure that you've given them a compelling **purpose** that provides meaning for everything they do. The right people are going to feel passionate about your purpose. They will believe strongly in what your company is trying to achieve, and that will give them a true north star to follow every single day.

And once you have the right people and the right purpose, then you need to provide them with **playbooks** that make your business repeatable and scalable. All that tribal knowledge and wisdom in the heads of your visionary leaders needs to be put down on paper. We're not talking about company policies or standard operating procedures, but a high-level checklist that ensures a repeatable experience for the customer or client.

When you have the right people, a great purpose, and playbooks for them to follow, you need to inspire **performance**. The question isn't "Do you have a Business Operating System?" The question is really "How well are you running your business?" Are you delivering on your promises? Are your employees able to deliver a predictable experience? Is your business scalable? Are you attracting and maintaining A-players? If you are performing well, A-players will want to be on your team. The fastest way to demotivate A-players is to surround them with poor performers.

If you focus on getting the right people, purpose, playbooks, and performance, the **profit** will follow. You can hit the ground running, and the money will take care of itself. You will wind up with a great war chest and the ability to invest in wonderful facilities, profit sharing, excellent pay and benefits for your people, and more. That, in essence, is the Pinnacle Path.

Can one person really make that much of a difference?

We see sports teams all the time that underperform even though, on paper, their roster tells you they should be winning.

The St. Louis Blues fired head coach Mike Yeo on November 20th, 2018. Craig Berube, the assistant coach, took over as interim head coach in his first year with the Blues. Sitting in last place in the NHL on January 3rd, the Blues went 30-10-5 for the rest of the year. Berube's team didn't just climb back into a playoff spot; they actually finished the regular season one point out of first place in the tough Central Division, and then dispatched the Winnipeg Jets, Dallas Stars, and San Jose Sharks in the playoffs before beating the Boston Bruins in seven games to win the championship.

The Blues general manager said Berube's success that season came from getting the players to focus on living in the moment. As Berube put it, "You're not going to change yesterday, and tomorrow's going to come soon enough. Let's work on today."

Berube said his approach revolves around accountability. "Whether it's through ice time or where you fit in the lineup, it takes a lot of work, every day. Once we started to get that and guys fitting in, in certain areas, conversations and holding players and people accountable, including myself, and putting the team first. When you do that and you have good players, you have a chance to win."[1] So, in this example, nothing changed except the head coach and how he approached his players. He was able to get them to "perform" at a much higher level with his systems and approach to coaching.

Bear in mind, the Pinnacle Path is intended for visionaries, big dreamers who want to grow their companies in amazing ways. If you run a small, simple business, then this may not be for you. Additionally, the way you go about this will depend entirely on the needs, objectives, and circumstances of your organization. There are many paths up the mountain, and you can pick the one that's best for you.

At the same time, you get the best of both worlds because Pinnacle still provides structure, discipline, a framework, and best practices, but you also have a much bigger toolbox and a freestyle approach. We're going to show you how to find the right path for your business so you can focus on people, purpose, playbooks, and performance no matter where you are as a business.

And as we said before, it all begins with your people.

---

1   Carol Schram, "Stanley Cup-Winning Coach Craig Berube Signs Three-Year Contract with St. Louis Blues," *Forbes*, June 26, 2019, https://www.forbes.com/sites/carolschram/2019/06/26/stanley-cup-winning-coach-craig-berube-signs-three-year-contract-with-st-louis-blues.

PRINCIPLE ONE

PEOPLE

"A-players are free, and they come with a financing option."

Building a company requires people, and people are mental, emotional, and physical beings. You can't treat them like cogs in a machine. Even cogs in a machine will break down if you don't take care of them or if you apply too much pressure. When *people* break, the consequences are usually severe. There are systems, tools, and processes you can use to help people get their work done on time, but you must prioritize their humanity by building intentional relationships and connections with them.

Sadly, we've seen some tragic examples of what happens when you don't take care of your people. None hit us harder than the story of Scott, a young, single father who finally reached his breaking point.

Scott's coworkers would later recall that he was a bit subdued that morning, perhaps a little quieter than usual, but they didn't think much of it. Of course, the people we work with every day are often a bit of a mystery. We don't always know what's going on in their personal lives, what they're dealing with, or how they really feel. Scott was close to a breaking point.

The company he worked for was a high-performance work environment. Once a quarter, leaders got together with their teams to check in and see how everyone was meeting their goals. The real purpose of these day-long quarterly sessions was to keep people on track and keep them accountable, so personal discussions were limited to a brief opening check-in question. At the very beginning of the meeting, leaders went around the room and asked each attendee to share some personal and professional "good news."

In reply, people would say things like:

"I watched my kid play hockey."

"I visited my in-laws in Peoria."

"The wife and I celebrated our anniversary with a dinner and a movie."

When the question was directed at Scott, he mentioned that he'd taken his daughter to the park. Scott was a single father, and his life mostly revolved around taking care of his only child. His answer to the opening question was very brief, but after all, it was a Monday morning. And we all know how stressful Monday mornings can be. You spend the weekend living your real life with your loved ones, doing what you want, but then it's back to the grind of "making a living."

What his colleagues didn't realize was that Scott's personal life was falling apart, and the high-pressure work environment was only compounding his anxiety and depression.

After the brief pleasantries, it was time to get down to business.

"Okay, let's see how everyone is doing at meeting their quarterly numbers," the facilitator said.

These quarterly meetings were supposed to be an opportunity to celebrate and reinforce the positive, but more often than not, leaders used them as a way to point out which team members were falling behind. And indeed, Scott had been falling behind on his goals for a while. He'd come to dread these meetings.

"Unfortunately, Scott, you missed your quarterly 'Rocks' *again*," the facilitator said. She could be very blunt, even ruthless, when confronting a performance issue, and she made sure Scott read the disapproval on her face.

"Sorry about that," Scott replied. "Things got a little out of control last quarter, but I feel good about the next several months. I'll keep trying to get things across the finish line."

"You missed your Rocks at the last quarterly session as well," the facilitator said, glaring sternly over the top of her reading glasses. "Scott, I feel like we should add your name to the 'list.'"

As Scott sat there, the facilitator walked to the front of the room and wrote his name in big, bold letters on a whiteboard beneath the heading "ISSUES." The list was a list of things that needed to be addressed that day to move the company forward.

Scott's heart sank. Suddenly, he felt like he was back in grade school, a little boy being singled out by his teacher for struggling with his reading lessons. His dyslexia had gone undiagnosed for years when he was young. Parents and teachers had often accused him of not trying hard enough when, in fact, Scott had been fighting hard to get good grades in the face of an immense personal challenge.

No one at the quarterly meeting knew about his childhood struggles or the ongoing pain he was dealing with. They just looked at him and saw an underperforming employee, and there was a prescribed approach to dealing with underperforming employees. When his name went up on the board, Scott got the message loud and clear. The shame and embarrassment he felt were overwhelming as he sat there all day long staring at his name, knowing that every other member of his team saw it as well. He felt judged, condemned.

You're the problem, Scott. That was the unspoken message. *You're the one dragging us down. It's because of you that this business can't meet its goals.*

He might as well have been wearing a dunce cap and sitting prominently on a stool. It was utterly humiliating, and on top of the constant stress of being a single father with very little support, the stress and strain were unbearable.

Somehow, Scott managed to hold it together. Indeed, he

expressed very little emotion that day, as his coworkers would later recount. After promising to do better during the upcoming quarter, he sat through the rest of the meeting without incident.

At the end of the day, after the all-day session finally came to an end, he said farewell to a couple of people and went home. As it turned out, getting publicly humiliated for his job performance was the last straw. He couldn't take it anymore. Once he was back at home, the stress and despair swept over him.

It's never going to get any better, he thought. *My personal life makes it impossible to perform at work, and my poor performance at work makes my personal life way more stressful. I'm caught in a downward spiral, and no one will help me.*

Seeing no way out, and no hope that things would ever improve, Scott took his own life that night.

When he failed to show up for work the next day, a coworker called his house. A distraught family member broke the news to her, and the coworker broke the news to the rest of the team. Everyone was shocked, and it became the talk of the office.

"How could this happen? He seemed okay yesterday, didn't he?"

"He seemed a little upset, but not to this extent."

"Did anyone see the warning signs?"

"He was behind on his quarterly goals, but I had no idea he was in such a bad place emotionally."

The leadership team couldn't believe it, but the truth is, they should have known. If they'd paid a little closer attention to the well-being of their team members, they would have noticed that the man was suffering, and perhaps they could have shown some real concern and compassion for him.

The leaders and coworkers wound up attending Scott's funeral, but the team was never quite the same. They carried the burden of that tragic incident with them for a long time. Hopefully, the hard lesson will make them a better and more compassionate team, but for Scott's daughter, his friends, and other loved ones, it was too late.

MAKE SURE EVERYBODY WINS

Scott's situation could have gone very differently. When the leadership team believes their people are their competitive advantage, inspires them with a purpose, and focuses on building a healthy culture and team that are all rowing in the same direction, amazing things happen all the time. In fact, Gregory knows of a man who was in a similar situation but received very different treatment from his leadership team, and it made all the difference.

At one of Gregory's sessions with a construction leadership team, Greg asked if anyone needed a shoutout for a job well done. A big burly operations manager (we'll call him "Tony") raised his hand and proceeded to tell us his story.

Like Scott, he'd found himself at a low point in his life. A single father, he was trying to raise his thirteen-year-old daughter all by himself, but financial woes due to past mistakes combined with a lack of a personal support network meant he was just barely keeping his head above water. Eventually, due to his financial problems, he found himself being forced to move out of his house.

It was a brutal turn of events. He'd built the house himself, but due to his circumstances, he'd wound up putting a mortgage on it. At the time, he'd desperately needed the money, so he felt like he had little choice.

Then he fell behind on payments, and the bank decided to foreclose on the property. Tony felt especially bad because his daughter was being forced to leave behind the only home she'd ever known. She'd had some hard years since losing her mother, and she struggled with anxiety at school. Her room was her safe space, and now she had to give it to someone else.

Listening to her cry broke his heart. And to top it all off, he only had until the weekend to get out of the house. With no help or support, Tony had no idea how they were going to get everything out of the house and relocated to their new rental in time. Much like Scott, he was overwhelmed, but as he went to work that week, he mostly kept all of this to himself.

Tony didn't like talking about his problems with his coworkers. He couldn't stand the idea of being pitied, so he just tried to keep his head down and get his work done. Coworkers and even the CEO noticed that he was quieter than usual. On top of that, his performance started to slip. Tony was usually very reliable and highly focused on the job, but he failed to complete some of his Rocks, and it was starting to affect the whole team.

Finally, the CEO Ryan pulled him aside and said, "Hey there, Tony, how are you doing? Is everything okay?"

"Oh, I'm fine," Tony replied. "Just thinking about some things."

"Are you sure?"

"Yeah, boss."

"Well, if you ever need to talk, let me know."

"I will," Tony said. "Don't worry about me."

But the weekend was closing in, and he still had no idea how he was going to make the move. He didn't have a truck to move their stuff, and he couldn't afford to rent one. His daughter was aware of this fact, and it only compounded her worry.

One evening, she asked him, "Dad, if we don't have a moving truck, does that mean we'll have to leave all of our stuff behind?" Tears in her eyes, she added, "Will I have to leave all of my books, my posters, and my furniture?"

"That's not going to happen," he said, trying to sound reassuring.

"But how are you going to get a truck?" she asked. "What are we doing to do?"

Tony had no answer for her, so just told her not to worry about it (knowing full well that she would). By Friday morning, desperation had set in. Finally, he made the reluctant decision to approach Ryan, the CEO of the company.

"Hey there, boss," he said timidly, stepping into the Ryan's big office. "I've got a little bit of a favor to ask of you. Do you think I could borrow a company box truck for tomorrow? My daughter and I are moving, and we must get it done this weekend."

"Wow, that's not a lot of time," Ryan replied. "Of course, you can borrow a truck, but this seems really sudden. Are you sure everything's okay?"

Tony hesitated a moment before saying, "You don't want to hear about my problems, boss."

"Sure I do," the CEO Ryan said. "I could tell you were stressed out about something all week. I want to help if I can. What's wrong?"

"It's a foreclosure," Tony explained. "The whole thing is my fault. I made some bad financial decisions. I've been fighting with the bank for months, and now I'm out of time. My poor daughter is heartbroken. She's afraid we'll have to leave all our stuff behind."

Ryan gave him a sympathetic smile and said, "I'll tell you what. Not only can you borrow a company truck, but I'll meet you here on Saturday and get you the truck myself."

It was the first real relief Tony had felt all week, so he thanked his boss profusely before returning to work. Later, he went home and broke the good news to his daughter. She would be able to take all her stuff with her! The company had come through for them.

When Tony showed up at the office on Saturday morning to

get the truck, the CEO, Ryan was there waiting for him, just as he'd promised. However, he'd brought along his two, strapping, college-age sons, as well.

"Tony, my friend," he said, "we're not only going to loan you a truck, but my sons and I are going to help you move. We'll make sure you get it done today!"

And indeed, they did. As Tony recounted the story later, they had everything moved into their new place by sunset on Saturday evening.

"My boss made a terrible situation so much better," he said. "I realized that weekend that Ryan really does care about his team as real people, not just employees. Even my daughter felt relieved knowing that someone had our back."

Gregory was present in the meeting when Tony shared this story, and it moved everyone to tears. No one else on the leadership team had heard the story until that moment. It may sound cliche, but there was such love in the room that day. Even the toughest guys were deeply moved.

As for Gregory, his prevailing thought was, *This CEO, Ryan, is exactly the kind of leader I want my kids to work for someday. What a great example of leadership for people to see!*

Tony, the operations manager, had such gratitude and loyalty to the company afterward that no company on earth could have recruited him away.

Compare a CEO like Ryan to a CEO who just wants to "tighten

the screws" to get people to work harder, regardless of what's going on in their personal lives. In the end, the compassionate CEO will get better performance and more engaged employees, and A-players will want to work for the company. Everybody wins.

If you don't have some means in place to clarify the well-being of your people and address their issues and struggles, then you're being reckless with your most important asset. Nothing in your company is more important than the people who work for you, and you need to treat them accordingly. If your people thrive, your business will thrive. It's as simple as that.

At Pinnacle Business Guides, we focus on building team health every time we meet with our clients, not just once a year at an annual retreat. Team health is something so important, so valuable, and so rare, that we believe it should be a focal point every time we come together as a team.

CHAPTER ONE

IT STARTS WITH THE RIGHT PEOPLE

We just said people are your biggest asset, but that's not entirely correct. If you have toxic people in your company, they are going to be far more of a liability than an asset. It's essential that you fill your company with A-players who believe in your culture and strive to deliver every day—the right people, in the right seats, doing the right things, and for the right reasons—*that's* when they become your biggest asset.

People are also your biggest investment, so why wouldn't you take the utmost care of them? Think about it. You spend most of your money not on rent, or trucks, or production, but on payroll. In almost every business, payroll is the biggest expense. Beyond the salary team members receive, there are also the benefits, payroll taxes, and other employee-related expenses.

Make sure your investment is well taken care of! This starts by making sure you hire the right people. In fact, as we like to say, "A-players are free." When you add the best people to your team, they are always going to put more value into the business than they take out.

Who are the A-players in your company right now? If you find it hard to answer that question, then try the following mental exercise. Imagine you were going to start your business all over again from scratch tomorrow. Who are the people at your company that you would absolutely take with you? That's your shortlist of A-players.

Typically, your A-players are people who share your values, work smart (not just *hard*), and strive to move your business forward every single day. Again, they do this not because you're constantly browbeating them (or publicly shaming them) but because you've hired the right people, created the right culture, and given them the tools and resources they need to excel.

When you don't have the right people on your team, you wind up spending a lot of energy trying to get people to do the work. You're constantly trying to create new processes, looking for some silver bullet that will transform B-players into A-players, but the end result is a lot of frustration that ends up hurting people and slowing down your business.

You must begin by hiring people who embrace your values and have the motivation to get things done. A-players occasionally come at a higher pay rate than industry norms, but the marginal value of having them on your team is always many times higher than the marginal cost of bringing them on board in place of a mediocre performer.

THE REAL VALUE OF A COMPETITIVE SALARY

The opening quote to Part One said, "A-players are free, *and they come with a financing option.*" What does that mean?

When an NFL team signs a superstar player, they give him a very lucrative, multi-year contract. For example, Aaron Rodgers signed a four-year deal with the Green Bay Packers in 2022 that was worth $200 million, which made him the highest-paid player in any position in the NFL. That lucrative, multi-year contract is intended to provide a powerful incentive for him to stick around and continue to perform at the highest level for multiple years.

Aaron Rodgers, like so many other professional sports players (with the exception of golfers), is paid based upon his *potential* not his *performance*, but like so many who get huge contracts, it doesn't guarantee that he will perform any better than before the contract.

When you hire A-players, you don't give them huge signing bonuses, pay them for their potential, or give them guaranteed contracts. Instead, you pay them market rate or a little above market rate. Every two weeks, you get to pay them *after* they have performed the work. You get to see their value first!

The reason we say the A-players are free is because if you look at that short list of the people you would take with you if you were starting over, you would probably agree that every single one of them is worth more to you and your business than what you pay them. And if you take care of them, they will be perfectly content to go above and beyond the call of duty. They will often come early and work late. They will show up on the weekend if necessary. Why? Because they feel well compensated, appreciated, encouraged, and inspired to always give their absolute best. You've given them the culture they need in order to thrive, and they thrive on achievement.

Sometimes, business leaders will think, "I can't afford to hire a top-notch, high-performing team member. I'll go broke trying to pay them a competitive salary." But the truth is, A-players always end up paying for themselves. They are *always* a good investment.

The Container Store is well-known for their commitment to hiring A-players. The co-founder of the company, Kip Tindell, famously said that a single A-player is worth three B-players. They achieved this not by creating a compassionless, high-stress environment where leaders grind people down in an effort to get better performance out of them. Rather, they began by paying people nearly twice the industry average. According to Tindell's book *Uncontainable*, the average Container Store retail salesperson was making nearly $50,000 a year by 2014, at a time when the national average for retail salespeople was just over $25,000.[2]

The thing is, paying an A-player above the market average is always going to be worth it, because they're going to create more value. As Tindell put it, "You can pay them twice as much and still save, since you get three times the productivity at two times the cost. They win, you save money, the customers win, and all the employees win because they get to work with someone great."[3]

But they didn't just throw money at people and then pull them into a hostile workplace. Rather, they sought out the very best people in retail and merchandising, compensated them well, *and* created an environment in which they could thrive.

WHO NOT HOW

Imagine a leader who possesses an incredible vision and a burning desire to achieve greatness. This leader, however, understands the limits of her own capabilities and recognizes the immense power in the collective strength of her team. Instead of obsessing over how she will personally accomplish every task and project, she shifts her focus to something even

2   Jenna Goudreau, "The Container Store CEO Shares His Best Advice for Small-Business Owners," Insider, November 25, 2014, https://www.businessinsider.com/container-store-ceo-best-advice-2014-11.

3   Aaron Taube, "Why the Container Store Pays Its Retail Employees $50,000 a Year," Insider, October 16, 2014, https://www.businessinsider.com/the-container-store-pays-employees-50000-a-year-2014-10.

more profound. She embarks on a quest to find the perfect "who" to entrust with tasks and projects that may not align with her own strengths and responsibilities.

She's in pursuit of that rare breed of talent—the A-player who possesses unwavering dedication, unmatched expertise, and an unquenchable thirst for excellence. She knows that by connecting these A-players with tasks that are ideally suited to their unique abilities, they will flourish and reach heights that would have been impossible for her to achieve alone.

As she empowers her A-players, she witnesses their growth and watches as they surpass even her own expectations. Together, they form an unstoppable force that propels the organization toward unprecedented success.

Who Not How is the art of recognizing and nurturing exceptional talent. When a leader lets go of the need to do it all herself and instead seeks out and finds the right "who," the stage is set for a successful climb to the top. Great people make all the difference.

Michael works with a client that creates "inspired restaurants" and has several fast-growing brands. When he started working with them in 2017, they had just ended the previous year with $36 million in revenue, and their flagship brand had seven locations across the Southwest. They had also just received an infusion of capital from a private equity firm.

Their executive team, made up primarily of people who had been with the company from the beginning, were attempting to ramp up and scale the business, but none of them had ever grown a business like this before. Their dream was to grow from seven to fifty-five locations, but that's hard to do when no one sitting around the executive table has ever done it and they're already being tapped out in terms of their capacity. To put it another way, it's difficult to map out a road you've never traveled.

Michael was brought on board to help, and as he began working with them, he helped them identify a major hindrance to growth: the people on their executive team. As much as the CEO loved the executive team members, they simply weren't able to scale themselves as fast as the company was capable of growing. Unfortunately, in many organizations, when leaders realize their team members aren't up to the task, they resist upgrading their teams. They think, "I don't want to be mean to them, hurt their feelings, or be disloyal," so they just keep trying to work with them.

In reality, though, you're not doing an employee any favors by keeping them around when they lack the skillset to meet your company's needs. You're just going to wind up grinding them down until they break. It's demoralizing when you're constantly being pushed hard to achieve something you're not equipped to achieve. Not only does it hold the company back, wasting time and resources, but it wears out the individuals who are under the constant pressure to perform beyond their abilities, skills, training, and comfort level.

So, the company was encouraged to do the most reasonable thing for everyone involved. Over the course of about two years, they completely rebuilt their executive team. They also brought in their first true Chief Financial Officer. Up to that point, they'd had a team member who operated as a VP of finance. She is still at the company, but she stepped into a different role to make room for a high-powered, highly skilled CFO who came from a restaurant group in San Francisco. It was a larger and more complex company than Michael's client, so the new CFO brought a set of skills and experience that were desperately needed.

The company also hired a new Chief Operating Officer who had been the executive director of food and beverage at a major Las Vegas hotel and casino and then senior vice president of restaurants and bars for a massive hotel company. Then they hired a new Chief Development Officer who had been senior vice president of real estate for a restaurant company with over 300 locations. Bear in mind, Michael's client had seven locations. They set a goal of fifty-five locations by the end of 2025, so the new CDO was more than prepared to make that growth happen. It's a road he already knew well.

Finally, they sought a new Chief Marketing Officer. The woman who had previously held that position was a great culture fit, which meant, among other things, that she was willing to *not* let her ego get in the way. She courageously stepped aside from leading the marketing team to take up a different position within the team. The woman they brought in as CMO had been director of marketing for a major snack food brand.

Now, they *could* have spent all of their time and money trying to grow their existing leadership team, mentoring them and pushing them in an effort to squeeze more performance out of them. When companies do this, they usually think they're doing the right thing. However, when you have the right people sitting in the wrong seats (or the wrong people sitting in the right seats), you usually just compound their misery by trying to tighten the screws, and as we said, it just slows your company down.

This was a great example of the CEO bravely confronting the brutal facts and making big and bold decisions to surround herself with an executive team of A-Players that was capable of guiding the organization not just in its present state but all the way to its summit of 55 locations.

As Gregory says, "Sometimes it's easier to change people than to change the people." So, the client made the wiser decision. They found the right people to sit around the executive table and brought them on board. As for the existing team members, in some instances, they were able to find more suitable positions for them elsewhere in the company; but in other cases, they were given generous severance packages and set free to find positions at other companies where they might continue to thrive.

"Sometimes it's easier to **change people** than to **change the people**."

As a guide for the company, Michael watched as the new team members, who brought with them a great culture fit combined with a more suitable skillset and more experience, transformed the executive team in amazing ways. Suddenly, individual leaders could be fully trusted to handle the tactical decision-making in their own individual areas of responsibility without needing constant help or oversight.

The team needed less tactical guidance from Michael. Quarterly meetings evolved to be less about handholding and "the system and tools" to quarterly strategy and performance. Organizational health-focused meetings now had completely customized agendas, where they would intensely stress-test their strategy, performance, and relationships. This amount of customization and evolution is often impossible with more rigid Business Operating Systems and coaches.

In terms of reaching their goals, putting the right people on the executive team made all the difference in the world. The company is now scaling and growing quickly, and as of the time of this writing, they are well over $100 million in revenue with twenty-one locations and a strong pipeline of real estate for the next eighteen months of openings. And it's all because their CEO was brave enough to "go big" on the people that she brought in to surround herself with.

What the client learned through this experience is that investing generously in the right people is always a smart investment. Conversely, keeping good people in the wrong seats is never doing anyone a favor. Get your people right, and you will get your company on the right track and reap the rewards that come from a smart investment.

Most companies are one leadership team away from either greatness or extinction. We could tell you stories about almost every single leadership team we've worked with in which a key leadership seat-change made an enormous impact over the course of our time with them. Remember, if you want to 5X the revenue and profit, you have to start with leveling up your leadership team.

A-PLAYERS MAKE ALL THE DIFFERENCE

One day, Gregory received a call from a client whose company belonged to an organization that represented more than 700 HVAC, electrical, and plumbing businesses across the country. Pinnacle works with between sixty to seventy HVAC clients, so it's an industry Gregory and the Pinnacle Business Guide community understands quite well.

This client had been in the heating and cooling business with his brothers for a long time, but recently he'd bought out the other brothers and taken control of the family business. Once his brothers were out, he built a new leadership team and then he tried to grow the business. A bunch of other people were chosen for various leadership roles, including a guy from finance who was appointed to be the second-in-command. That particular individual proved to be a nightmare, impossible to please and relentlessly critical to those working under him.

He would show up and never have the numbers for the past quarter or the future quarter. If the team got ninety-nine things right, he focused on the one thing they missed. He was the type of person who, if he were grading something on a scale of one-to-ten or A-to-F, would say, "I never give tens or A's because there's always room for improvement." The rest of the leadership team didn't respect him or want to work for this owner-appointed second-in-command.

Overall, the leadership team proved to be a disaster. Almost nobody was in the right seat. They didn't have the right sales leader, or marketing leader, or HR leaders. None of them were A-players. The company lost a million dollars in a single quarter, and suddenly the founder was in meltdown mode. All that he'd hoped for, the growth that he'd thought he might achieve, was totally undone simply by selecting leaders who weren't A-players and weren't the right fit.

When Gregory was brought on board, one of his priorities was to help them rebuild the leadership team. He identified certain individuals on the leadership team who were simply unable to get the job done. Some of them had twenty years of experience, but they couldn't tackle the problems the company was facing.

One by one, Greg helped the founder bring in the right people to take over positions of leadership in the company. Some A-players were hiding in plain sight, including one talented individual who had been with the company for seventeen years in various capacities. Gregory recognized that he was an undervalued player, so the owner made him second-in-command, taking the place of the original pick.

Within a year, they found A-players for every seat on the leadership team, and the company went from losing a million dollars in a quarter to *making* a million dollars plus in a quarter. Even during the pandemic of 2020 to 2021, the new leaders came together to protect the jobs of their employees and keep the company thriving.

Here's the thing, you don't always know when you have the wrong people on your team. Sometimes, they *seem* like the right people, but once you bring in a few A-players, the difference becomes crystal clear. They may not have the most industry experience; they may not have the right degree. But when you get an A-player on your team, it's going to be an amazing upgrade.

With his new team, the client's company is now making more progress than ever, and the owner went from not being able to take a vacation to taking his family on trips even in peak season. His leadership team has also created a better culture, making bigger, bolder decisions, and it all started by creating a cohesive leadership team of A-players. That's the *only* thing that changed. Getting A-players on the leadership team is the *one thing* we focused on, and it made all the difference. Who on your leadership team is in the wrong seat?

LET THEM RUN

Once you hire A-players, you have to let them run. Give them plenty of room to lead, and they will accomplish amazing things. They will surprise you, solving big challenges that have kept you up at night for a long time. It's worth it to pay them generously. The ROI of an A-player is always worth the investment!

If you can get just one A-player in a key position in your company, it's going to make all the difference. They will start having an impact from day one.

CHAPTER TWO

THE IMPORTANCE OF CLEAR EXPECTATIONS

"The beatings will continue until morale improves!"

Even if the boss doesn't say it explicitly, this is the attitude of leaders at some companies, but there's never a need for threats or scolding when you have A-players on your team. You won't find yourself trying to squeeze more performance out of them because they will achieve amazing things and have fun doing it.

Earlier, you were encouraged to figure out who the A-players are on your team. Business Operating Systems sometimes have basic tools that enable you to categorize whether or not people fit with each of your core values, but they don't necessarily help you to acutely assess their ability to perform their role. These kinds of tools will show you if someone is a good culture fit and if they are capable of performing in their role, but they don't reveal who the A-players are. Additionally, they don't always provide any empirical data that allows people to focus on consistently improving their performance.

It's always emotionally challenging to sit down with an employee to have a conversation about how their behavior doesn't align with your culture or how their performance fails to meet expectations. However, the conversation will always be more fruitful when you can identify areas where they excel and areas where they are falling behind, rather than simply reprimanding them across the board for vague problems.

Some leaders avoid these kinds of uncomfortable conversations altogether, but we feel that if you can use a tool that provides empirical data on how an employee is doing in different areas, then it sets the table to have a more productive interaction.

The fact is most employees *want* to know which specific areas they can concentrate on in order to improve their performance. They *crave* clarity on their expectations, so they can improve and perform at a high level. What they don't want is vague, nonspecific browbeating, a lack of clarity about what is expected of them, or no real sense of how they can improve their performance.

"I don't know what I'm doing wrong. I don't know how to get better. But the person I directly report to is always upset with me." That's the kind of thing that decimates morale.

A-PLAYER TALENT ASSESSMENT

To fill this gap, Pinnacle has adopted a people tool called the Talent Assessment, a tool inspired by a system called Topgrading, which has been around since 1997.[4] With the Talent Assess-

---

4   Bradford D. Smart and Geoffrey H. Smart, "Topgrading the Organization," *Directors & Boards* (Spring 1997): 22–28, https://www.directorsandboards.com/articles/singletopgrading-organization.

ment, each employee is evaluated by the person they report to, measuring how well they live and exemplify the culture, and measure their productivity on how well they deliver results for their specific role with a score. The following instructions are given for the company's core values.

TALENT ASSESSMENT EXERCISE

- **Step 1:** Enter the initials of your team members.
- **Step 2:** For each team member, assign their Cultural Fit Score (0–10) based on how well they live and exemplify your culture.
- **Step 3:** Assign their Productivity Score (0–10) based on how well they deliver results for their specific role.
- **Step 4:** Plot them on the graph.

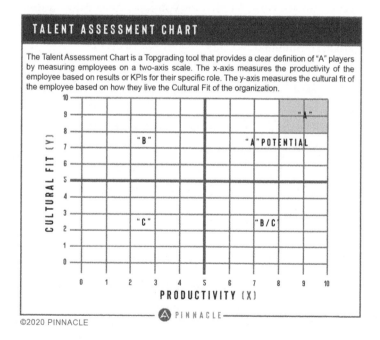

TALENT ASSESSMENT CHART

The Talent Assessment Chart is a Topgrading tool that provides a clear definition of "A" players by measuring employees on a two-axis scale. The x-axis measures the productivity of the employee based on results or KPIs for their specific role. The y-axis measures the cultural fit of the employee based on how they live the Cultural Fit of the organization.

©2020 PINNACLE · PINNACLE

This provides very specific feedback that identifies your A-players, and it also leads to better conversations. You can quickly see how many of your people are A-players, A-potential, B-players, and so on. You should take action on the C-players right away because they are hurting your culture and performance.

Our role as leaders in companies is to coach and mentor people "up and to the right" on this chart. We love to see people go from a B or B/C player to an A-potential, and better yet, we love to see more people become A-players. A measure of a great leader is that they can consistently grow and develop people. If people are not all-in on your culture, is it them or is it the fact that you don't have a clear vision of the culture you want for your company? Do you lack a vision of what "good" looks like? What are you doing to help people weigh-in and buy into your culture? As for productivity, do you have clear expectations around the quality of work? If not, it's going to be hard to hold them accountable.

This is a simple chart that is designed to have an "Aha!" effect because it provides a striking visual for seeing your team. And this is the team you are putting out in the marketplace to win business away from the competition. We've seen instances where an entire department, including the department leader, were *not* in the "A-player" box. If the leaders are not A-players, they probably won't hire people who are better than they are.

WORKING WITH CLARITY ON PEOPLE

There are Business Operating Systems whose processes are designed to stop working with a client after a certain number of months. One such company came to a Pinnacle Business

Guide after they had graduated from their Business Operating System, and it soon became clear that there was a lot of confusion around employee performance and culture fit. They'd put some foundational elements in place and made some incremental improvements, but they were struggling to gain clarity on how their people were doing.

We introduced them to the Talent Assessment tool, and all of a sudden, a bright light was being shined on a variety of people issues.

Imagine suddenly being able to put a quantifiable number on how a team member is doing in embracing your culture and their job performance, and doing so in relationship to other members of the team. With this data, we were able to create a matrix that showed graphically the relative position of each employee. The A-players, B-players, and C-players were crystal clear, and the information was actionable.

The leaders of the company looked at the graph and had a startling realization. They had some people with performance gaps who had been hiding off the radar because they didn't have enough data to spot them or address problem areas. Now, they knew exactly who to coach and what the performance gaps were. It was revolutionary and led to significant performance improvements. This, in turn, resulted in major growth for the company.

Once you've plotted your entire team on the Talent Assessment, ask yourself where you and your leaders spend the most time: with your A-players or the B and B/C players.

Where should you be spending your time for the greatest return?

CHAPTER THREE

MAINTAINING A HIGH-PERFORMING HEALTHY TEAM

Your success begins with your people. If you don't provide your employees with a great experience, then your customers aren't going to have a great experience. You can't mistreat your people and expect them to treat customers well.

That means your people are your greatest strategic advantage. So, when you adopt the attitude, "I'll pay them just enough to make them show up to work," your employees are going to respond, "Okay, then I'll do just enough work to avoid getting fired." And this is the game that's being played all the time out there in the business world.

It doesn't have to be this way. You can pay your people the top rates in the industry if you hire more A-players, because A-players produce twice or three times as much as B- and C-players. Change your mindset about your people. Get A-players on your team; give them the right tools, direction, and vision; and pay them generously. Amazing things will happen.

They will go above and beyond the call of duty. They will solve problems and figure out better answers. And they'll have a blast doing it. You can't get rich by demand. You can't simply threaten people to produce more widgets. The dictatorial leadership style is a relic of the past. The world has changed, and people are no longer willing to sacrifice their entire life and lifestyle, including time with friends and loved ones, just to get a paycheck.

In an age of artificial intelligence and automation, your people can become your greatest strategic advantage, so make sure you're connected to them. Make sure you understand them and know who they are. Are you giving them the tools they need to be successful? It starts with your leadership team. Your leaders need to be better at leading next year than they are this year. The bottleneck is at the top of the bottle so that's where the change must begin.

To start with, stop seeing your people as your biggest expense, your biggest liability, your biggest pain. Instead, start seeing them as your greatest opportunity. Focus on building a team of great people. As Patrick Lencioni said in his book *The Five Dysfunctions of a Team*, "If you could get all the people in the organization rowing in the same direction, you could dominate any industry, in any market, against any competition, at any time."[5]

Once you have the right people on your team, with the right

---

5   Patrick Lencioni, *The Five Dysfunctions of a Team: A Leadership Fable* (New York: Jossey-Bass, 2002), vii.

resources, you must give them a purpose that will inspire their best performance at all times. As the old proverb goes, "Without vision, the people perish." If you're a parent, then you know how important it is sometimes to give your kids a purpose, especially for activities that they don't enjoy. If you give them a compelling purpose, then they're more likely to commit to the activity with enthusiasm.

"Mom, why do I have to get good grades at school?"

"So you can learn and grow and get your dream job when you grow up."

The need for a purpose doesn't end with childhood. A compelling purpose carries people through the rough patches and adversities. A meaningful "why" unlocks an A-player's potential. Next, we'll look at how you can create a compelling purpose for everything your people do.

GENEROSITY LEADS TO GROWTH

Bob had worked his whole life for billion-dollar companies in the construction industry, but he finally started his own business. When he started working with a Pinnacle Business Guide, he had twenty-five employees, and he was doing about $20 million a year in revenue. Bob set out to find real A-players to add to his team. He wanted the very, very best people, but that meant he had to recruit some people away from other companies.

To do that, he had to navigate through a few noncompete clauses, even as he put them on the payroll. Ultimately, he hired one of the best general superintendents in the industry, and some of the best development, project managers, and others. As a result of the change in leadership, his business grew from $20 million to $100 million. And now, years later, it's a $300 million company that has won multiple "best places to work" awards.

By adding some of the best people in the industry to his leadership team, he has created one of the hundred-largest privately-owned companies in Minneapolis. It is the quintessential story of "hockey stick" growth, a meteoric rise that resulted from one simple change: getting the right people.

More than that, he has created a stellar company culture. He is exceedingly generous with his team. They have a tradition of closing down the entire office on the Friday before Labor Day to take every employee and their families to the Minnesota State Fair. He does these kinds of things all the time. Bob is a great human being, and he understands the importance of his people. He's the kind of guy who would fire a client before he fired the trade partner.

If clients are beating up on his people, other leaders might say, "The customer is always right." But Bob has no problem calling an abusive client and saying, "If you verbally assault my project manager again, we will come over there to the worksite, grab all of our tools, and walk off the job." Practically speaking, he knows that if he takes care of his people first, they will take care of the customers.

INVESTING IN FUTURE LEADERS

One of Michael's clients is a specialty burger and beer chain with more than forty locations that offer all kinds of different meats, toppings, and preparations. Each of their locations is led by a general manager, and every year, the company takes all of their general managers, plus their supporting teams, on a long weekend retreat for leadership and team building.

Leveling up employees is common in many industries, but especially in the restaurant industry. You might start as a server or bartender, but if you do a good job and show leadership potential, you will eventually find yourself being elevated. Indeed, most general managers in restaurants started out as entry-level employees.

The problem is many companies level up their employees without investing enough in teaching them the "soft skills" of leadership. Consequently, many general managers don't know how to adapt or meet people where they are. They don't know how to coach or develop their own employees, which often results in a dictatorial style of leadership.

To prevent this, Michael's client invests a tremendous amount of time, money, and resources in training their general managers to see themselves not as "managers" but as "leaders." They teach them the soft leadership skills that help them build effective relationships with their employees. Leadership retreats are designed to be *experiential* and *memorable*, so they select unique, intimate venues. In the past, these have included luxury tents on the beach in Mendocino, California, and a ranch complex in Rocky Mountain National Park.

The goal is to create emotional moments that bind the team together while also teaching valuable leadership skills, so they include unusual activities like having a traveling troubadour play live music wherever they go. It might sound odd, but they want their people to feel like they are connected to a team of like-minded people around a bigger purpose.

They call it the Leadership Conference and the theme is "Connect, Ignite, and Grow," which means *connecting* with one another, *igniting* the drive to live out their core values and make a positive impact in their restaurants, and *grow* as human beings and leaders. In other words, they're not just focused on tactical growth, but also on personal development.

Beyond leadership training, they have a compensation plan called "512." When a general manager has been with the company for **five** years, they get a **one**-year salary bonus, so if someone is making $80,000 a year, they get a check for $80,000 at the end of year five. They also get a **twenty-eight-day** sabbatical that they can use to spend time with family or do whatever they want.

The combination of this kind of engagement with this level of investment allows them to set a higher bar for managers. They give more, so they can expect more. It's a great example of the saying, "If you want to 5X your business, you have to 5X your people."

We now have several clients who offer sabbaticals as a way to reward and keep A-players. It can be as simple as a month off to do what you want, and you don't have to be a large company to do this. We have clients who are less than $10 million in revenue that have had people take sabbaticals this year and come back refreshed, renewed, and ready for the next summit they will be climbing.

What can you do to become a destination for top talent in your industry? Hint: for A-players, it's not offering two weeks' vacation plus six holidays on the way in.

THE PEOPLE PRINCIPLE: ACTIONS TO TAKE

- A-players always put more value into the business than they take out. They get the job done and move your business forward every single day, so you can afford to compensate them generously.

- Get A-players on your team; give them the right tools, direction, and vision; pay them generously; and give them plenty of room to lead. They will accomplish amazing things.

- Your company may be one leadership team away from either greatness or extinction.

- Employees want to know which specific areas they can concentrate on in order to improve their performance. They crave clarity on their expectations, so they can improve and perform at a high level.

- Your success begins with your people. If they don't have a great experience, then your customers aren't going to have a great experience.

PURPOSE

"Life is never made unbearable by circumstances, but only by lack of meaning and purpose."

—VIKTOR FRANKL

Work often feels like a just four-letter word, especially when it's devoid of an inspiring purpose. The reason why so many people show up late, slog through the day, and daydream about leaving is because their work feels like drudgery. It feels like they're getting paid to do a job that doesn't really matter. In the absence of an inspiring purpose, even a complex job can feel like a glorified version of pressing a single button on a factory floor over and over again, day after day.

But when you have an inspiring purpose, that very same work feels entirely different to the same people because they now see a greater value in what they're doing. When you can tap into a meaningful purpose, you can find the motivation and inspiration to work hard and give it your best. Think of an ICU nurse working seven days a week during the pandemic because she's trying to help combat the disease and save lives. When she understands her purpose, suddenly her job seems like more than a job, and the hard work seems like more than mere work.

You can do the same with any job. A person on a factory line putting together electrical harnesses can feel like they're part of a greater purpose. Maybe the harnesses are a vital part of machines that help save lives. Suddenly, that worker can see the real value in what they're doing day in and day out. They are contributing to something that matters, not just earning a paycheck.

TO THE MOON

In the early days of NASA, the organization struggled because they lacked a clearly defined, singular goal, but all of that changed when President John F. Kennedy gave his famous speech on September 12, 1962. "We choose to go to the moon in this decade and do the other things," he declared, "not because they are easy, but because they are hard, because that goal will serve to organize and measure the best of our energies and skills, because that challenge is one that we are willing to accept, one we are unwilling to postpone, and one which we intend to win, and the others, too."[6]

---

6   "Address at Rice University on the Nation's Space Effort, September 12, 1962," John F. Kennedy Presidential Library and Museum, accessed January 30, 2023, https://www.jfklibrary.org/archives/other-resources/john-f-kennedy-speeches/rice-university-19620912.

The idea of putting a man on the moon and safely returning him to the earth became the driving purpose of all of NASA's efforts, and it made a huge difference. From that point on, you could ask any single NASA employee anywhere in the company the reason for the work they did, and they would tell you, "I'm helping put a man on the moon."

Why was the janitor cleaning floors in NASA's building? Because it was his contribution to putting a man on the moon. "I'm cleaning floors so people can move around safely in here and do the hard work they need to do to get that rocket to the moon," he might have said. Indeed, 300,000 people relocated their families to Houston and Cape Canaveral in order to become part of NASA's race to the moon. The president's inspiring purpose motivated them to get behind this big, crazy idea.

Some worked on propulsion, some worked on navigation, and others worked on life support. But they all had one thing that united them: a bold purpose. Isn't this really the goal of life? Find your true calling, your real passion, and then devote your talents, skills, and efforts toward realizing it. That calling might be delivering financial services, manufacturing products, constructing buildings, or something else, but you'll gladly devote your efforts toward it. And as a side effect, you get to call it "work."

That's when work doesn't feel like work. That's when the hours seem to pass by quickly, too quickly, and people sometimes need to tell you, "Go home already. It's late!" When a dedicated team in a lab is trying to cure cancer, they're not watching the clock and waiting for their shift to end. Sometimes, you might even find them sleeping on the floor in the lab because they feel like they're close to a breakthrough. Their "job" is their life's work, far more than a way to pay the bills.

THE STOCKDALE PARADOX

Admiral Jim Stockdale was the highest-ranking US military officer held in the "Hanoi Hilton" prison camp during the Vietnam War. During his imprisonment, he was tortured twenty times. For eight years, he was held in that prison, with no idea if he would ever be released, as he endured brutal conditions. Holidays came and went, months turned into years, and his suffering continued.

During that period, he saw many other prisoners of war give up hope and die, but as he said in an interview, "I never doubted not only that I would get out, but also that I would prevail in the end and turn the experience into the defining event of my life…" And indeed, he was eventually freed from the Hanoi Hilton in 1973.

Nevertheless, when asked about the prisoners who gave up hope and died over the years, he said they were the optimists. "The optimists. Oh, they were the ones who said, 'We're going to be out by Christmas.' And Christmas would come, and Christmas would go. Then they'd say, 'We're going to be out by Easter.' And Easter would come, and Easter would go. And then Thanksgiving, and then it would be Christmas again. And they died of a broken heart."

It might seem like a contradiction. After all, wasn't Stockdale himself an optimist? He was convinced that he would be set free, and he hung in there for eight years, never giving up hope of eventually getting out of that hellhole.

Stockdale makes this important distinction: "You must never confuse faith that you will prevail in the end—which you can never afford to lose—with the discipline to confront the most brutal facts of your current reality, whatever they might be."[7]

In other words, the optimists had hope of release, but they also refused to confront the harsh reality that they might have to face more hardship before that happened. And that was what led to their downfall. Stockdale, on the other hand, was absolutely convinced that someday he would be set free, but he was also willing to accept the possibility that it was going to be a long, brutal road to freedom. Be convinced of success but confront the hard road you must take to get there. This is called the Stockdale Paradox.

If you can adopt the attitude that Admiral Stockdale had, then you have enough hope to succeed without the naivete to assume it will be quick or easy.

A similar story is told by Holocaust survivor Lily Ebert, who was twenty when she first arrived at Auschwitz concentration camp. As recounted in a series of TikTok videos, some of which have gained millions of views, "In Auschwitz, you were not afraid of death; you were afraid to live." Yet somehow, she survived brutal conditions long enough to be liberated on January 27, 1945.

While people gave up hope and died around her in the camp, she endured, and she attributes her survival, in large part, to her attitude. As she put it, "I promised myself, however long I will be alive, and whatever I will do in life, one thing is sure,

---

7   "The Stockdale Paradox," JimCollins.com, accessed January 30, 2023, https://www.jimcollins.com/concepts/Stockdale-Concept.html.

I will tell my story."[8] That drive and determination to tell her story gave her just enough hope to keep going, even in the face of a harsh reality.

What does this have to do with running or leading a business? Lily Ebert and James Stockdale went through horrifying ordeals that most of us will never experience even in our worst nightmare. However, their survival stories tell us something about the human condition that is relevant even to being an effective business leader. The people who make it have a conviction that they are going to reach their desired goal, but they don't ignore or overlook the hardships they will endure to get there.

This is a reality of human achievement that can be seen at all levels of experience, from the most mundane situations to the most extraordinary or extreme. Every employee in your company needs to have some inspiring purpose that they are working toward, with a strong conviction that they can and will achieve that purpose, but they must also understand that it's going to take hard work to get there.

RALLY THE TROOPS

With that in mind, let's look at some important elements of creating a compelling purpose that will "rally the troops." First, you need to clearly define the "why" for your company. Why do you exist, and why does it matter? Remember, you're not looking for some "one-size-fits-all" purpose that could be applied

---

8   Maria Pasquini, "98-Year-Old Holocaust Survivor Is Keeping Her Promise to Tell Her Story—And She's Doing It on TikTok," *People*, January 27, 2022, https://people.com/ human-interest/98-year-old-holocaust-survivor-lily-ebert-telling-story-on-tiktok/.

to any business, but something that is uniquely suited to your industry and organization.

Once you have that purpose, you need to strategize differently, so you understand how your company stands apart from every other business in your industry or market. Finally, you need to create and articulate a powerful brand message, both internally and externally.

But it all starts with your "Just Cause."

CHAPTER FOUR

WHAT'S YOUR "JUST CAUSE"?

In his book *The Infinite Game*, Simon Sinek talks about the importance of clarifying your vision of a future state, something you believe in at your core that doesn't currently exist—and perhaps never fully will—a vision that is so inspiring, you're willing to commit your entire career toward its advancement. Sinek calls that your "Just Cause."[9]

Take, for example, the United States' Declaration of Independence, which was written in 1776. It begins with a relatively short statement that proposes a belief in a future state where, "all men are created equal...endowed by their Creator with certain unalienable Rights...among these are Life, Liberty and the pursuit of Happiness."

The idea that one day every human being will be truly viewed as equal, that every single person will have full and free right to life, liberty, and the pursuit of happiness, is an inspiring vision. Sadly,

---

9   Simon Sinek, *The Infinite Game* (Edmonton, Alberta: Portfolio, 2019).

it may never be fully realized, but it's a vision that inspired the founding fathers and many others to risk their fortunes, their lives, their families, and more to go to war.

According to Sinek, a "Just Cause," when you understand it, becomes the North Star for every decision you make going forward. Indeed, the vision presented in the Declaration of Independence continued to inspire future generations to fight hard to realize it more fully. That vision drove the abolition of slavery. It drove the fight for women's suffrage, the Civil Rights movement, and more.

We continue to see groups of people pushing toward the future state described in the Declaration of Independence, trying to get us closer to the fullness of it. Compare that to the many nations where people are persecuted, even executed, for being different than the majority of the population. That's the power of a "Just Cause."

CLARIFYING A CORE FOCUS

Michael recently started working with a coffee roasting and retail company that also has coffee shop locations in multiple states. One of the biggest frustrations the leaders of the company had before they started working with Michael was the constant struggle to get their employees to embrace the whole idea of their operating system. Their team just wouldn't fully engage, and as a result, they weren't getting the value they had hoped for.

While it made sense and worked well at the leadership level, leaders couldn't figure out how to drive it to be embraced at lower levels of the organization. Leaders were unable to tell a good story that communicated the purpose of a Business Operating System effectively. They had clarified what they called their Core Focus™ (purpose and niche), so they felt like they had checked all of the right boxes. However, no one had ever shown them how to build a compelling story around their purpose.

Michael encouraged them to elevate their thinking and identify a "Just Cause," as defined by Sinek. He had a long conversation with the founders of the coffee company and encouraged their executive team to begin sharing ideas freely. He wanted to see what common words and phrases they would use as they talked about their company's purpose and how that supported a greater Just Cause. As he identified these words and phrases, he wrote them on a whiteboard.

From there, Michael began helping them piece together their "Just Cause" and purpose, and from there he taught them how to follow a storytelling framework to create their own unique and inspiring story about it. Essentially, it was the story of a coffee company that sourced green coffee directly from Guatemala, where they'd built relationships with local farmers. It talked about how much philanthropic work the company is doing with these third-world farmers and their farms. This connected the end product to an ongoing process of making life better for the people of Guatemala and the people in their own communities.

They ended up with a "Just Cause" that they find highly inspiring and very true to their beliefs and vision for the future. They have evolved their storytelling to be much more emotional and impactful in helping their employees understand the purpose behind what they do and how they do it. When employees can connect the dots to something bigger, they often bring more energy, creativity, and focus to their work.

At the time of this writing, that company has ten locations in places like Palm Springs, Phoenix, Tucson, and Austin, and they are opening two more locations very soon (with several more on the horizon). Their "Just Cause" has given a compelling purpose to the work of every individual in the company at every level.

In fact, the company has become so enamored with fulfilling their "Just Cause" that they're actually working on becoming a B Corp, which is defined as a company that meets higher standards for performance, accountability, and transparency in regard to things like charitable giving and supply chain practices. They are very community-focused, and each of their locations tries to bring positive change to the communities in which they operate.

CHANGE THE NARRATIVE

A high-level, aspirational, inspirational purpose told as a compelling story about the origin and "Just Cause" of the company has become a powerful tool for communicating purpose to every employee. And leaders are finding that the people working in their stores resonate emotionally with that story. They feel connected to it.

That, in turn, makes it much easier to understand the importance of things like their Functional Accountability Chart, why clarity about roles matters, why coaching conversations and mentor meetings are important, why tracking data matters, and so on. Now, instead of seeing something like profit and cash flow as merely benefiting the owner, they see it as fueling a reinvestment in advancing their "Just Cause."

Having a "Just Cause" changed the narrative of the entire company all the way down to the frontlines of the organization. While it took a lot of thought, work, and refinement to get it just right, the end result was a succinct statement that they could be proud of, and a clear and compelling story behind it that helped team members emotionally connect with their vision for the organization and the future.

CHAPTER FIVE

HOW WILL YOU STRATEGIZE DIFFERENTLY?

We live in a world that is doing its best night and day to make you just like everyone else. If an innovative idea comes out on the East Coast, it will quickly be adopted on the West Coast, and then it will spread to the rest of the country. A trendy regional dish in one city will become a trendy dish in all cities. A song that becomes a local hit will eventually become a national hit. We listen to the same things, eat the same things, wear the same things, and watch the same things.

And that pressure toward homogenization impacts the decisions of business leaders. We often default to doing what we think we're supposed to do based on what every other successful business in our space is doing.

When you're just doing what everyone else does, the only way to compete is through pricing, and that's a race to the bottom.

Eventually, you find yourself charging the same as everyone else and trying to survive with razor-thin margins.

Figure out how your company is going to strategize differently. What are you going to do that will make you stand out from the crowd in your industry or niche? Clarify your "differentiating activities," and your uniqueness will soon become clear.

NOTICE ME!

If you decided today that you were going to open a fitness gym, what would your strategy be? Chances are, you'd rent a 30,000-square-foot space, fill it with plenty of gym equipment, offer one-year memberships, charge a monthly fee, and then stay open twenty-four hours a day. That's what all the big, successful gyms do. LA Fitness, Life Time Fitness, Planet Fitness, FitnessOne—take your pick. Why wouldn't you want to be just like them?

The problem is, though, if you don't do things differently, no one is going to hear you shouting, "Notice me," in a crowded marketplace where there are plenty of bigger, louder voices. If you follow the same strategy as everyone else, how are you going to entice people to give your new business a chance?

This is the struggle that one of Greg's clients faced when he founded his chain of boutique fitness centers in 2006. He realized early on that he needed a strategy that made his business stand out from the crowded world of fitness gyms. He didn't want to simply follow the trends, and as you probably know, fitness trends come and go, whether you're talking about hot yoga, goat yoga, or Peloton. He wanted a business strategy that made his company truly unique and attractive.

Greg met him in 2013, and at the time, he had three locations. Greg encouraged him to identify a list of "differentiating activities" that would make his company stand out. He enthusiastically embraced this approach and began looking for ways to set himself apart. Unlike the big 30,000-square-foot gyms, he decided not to try to be all things to all people. First, he began by establishing a few basics, such as 1) always giving customers a warm welcome and a fond farewell, 2) maintaining surgically clean facilities, and 3) using evidence-based fitness that relied on the latest research.

Then, he decided to target a different crowd. His company would be designed for the six-figure professional living in a nice house in the suburbs, the kind of person who doesn't want to work on their fitness while surrounded by a gym full of muscleheads. Instead of 30,000-square-foot gyms filled with equipment, he built 1,000-square-foot micro-studios that appealed to people who only wanted to come twice a week and pay $59 for a thirty-minute session. And he created a strength-training program based on the most efficient, evidence-based fitness routines.

Additionally, unlike most fitness gyms, he decided that there would be no membership. Customers don't have to sign up for a year at a time. This makes sense because, after all, if a customer isn't happy with their experience, they're not going to come back anyway, so why lock them into a contract? That only breeds resentment.

He upped the minimum requirements for trainers and increased their pay. At most fitness gyms, trainers need little more than a basic certification. They don't do any practical training, and they end up making about $15 an hour. He changed all of that.

Beginning trainers now required a four-year degree in kinesiology or physiology, and he began hiring them right out of college. With a creative and aggressive compensation plan, high performers could earn up to $90,000 a year.

From the experiences they created for customers to the way they set up their facilities, hired trainers, and treated their employees, everything about the company changed. The founder and his team came up with a strategy that made his business stand out in the marketplace. Growth soon followed. He opened a fourth location, then a fifth, sixth, and seventh, and each location began generating far more profit. At the time of this writing, they are well on their way to their hundredth location, and that growth is largely due to his determination to be different.

In an industry filled with multi-billion-dollar companies all doing roughly the same thing, he identified an underserved market and found a profitable niche. Since most new gyms follow the same strategy as the biggest players in the industry, there's really nothing to set them apart. And that's exactly why so many of the smaller places don't last. They lack a clear strategy to differentiate, so they fail to ever scale the business.

This fitness company stands out in almost every way, and that attracts the people who are in their target market. Rather than fading into the noise caused by a crowded industry, their distinctions make them hugely attractive to the right people—and that's a recipe for success.

CHAPTER SIX

TELLING A POWERFUL BRAND STORY

People aren't going to figure out what makes you unique on their own. You must tell them *how* you're different, and *why* you're different. And if your differentiators are valuable, people will pay more for your products and services. If you lack a good strategy for differentiating yourself, then your execution doesn't matter, and no one can help you. You're going to be relegated to a commodity—and lots of competition!

It's not enough to share some facts or statistics about your company's achievements. You need to create a narrative that shares your brand's history, successes, and value propositions in a way that sets you apart from every other brand—and makes you unique so no one else can duplicate what you're doing.

According to cognitive psychologist Jerome Bruner, people are 22 times more likely to remember a fact when it's wrapped in a story.[10] If you can tell people a great story about who you are, a story that makes you unique in your industry, then people will notice and remember you. More than that, when customers interact with your company, it will feel like more than a mere transactional relationship.

This is an area where many clients struggle in the world of Business Operating Systems. They don't take enough time to look at their brand and brand promises. They don't really understand how they're going to be different, or what their unique story is going to be. They try to be all things to all people, and as a result, they don't really know who they are.

In the absence of a great brand story, you tend to compete on prices. But competing on price, as we've said, is a downward spiral. Before you know it, you no longer have any margin to invest in marketing, branding, training, or development.

When you're crystal clear about who you are, what you stand for, and where you're going, then decision-making becomes so much easier. More than that, when you turn that into an inspiring brand story, it gives purpose to every single person who works for you and creates a deep emotional connection with everyone who does business with you.

LIVE OUT YOUR STORY

When Michael helped the coffee roasting company identify a "Just Cause," he did more than just help them discover a purpose. He also helped them turn that purpose into a compelling

---

10   "The Science of Stories: How Stories Impact Our Brains," Quantified, April 2, 2018, https://www.quantified.ai/blog/the-science-of-stories-how-stories-impact-our-brains/.

brand message that they can share both internally and externally. Some companies do this really well.

In fact, you might be surprised that companies in certain industries are able to create really compelling brand stories. In Chapter 3, we mentioned our friend Bob, who runs a general contracting business in Minneapolis. Bob has created a fascinating brand story for his company that truly sets them apart in the commercial construction industry.

How did he do it? By positioning his brand as a "hospitality company" that just happens to operate in the commercial construction industry. The company frames their general contracting services as a means of helping their clients be the best at who they want to be by designing spaces that meet their needs and reflect their personality. And, as their website declares, they are committed to giving clients a great experience throughout the project.

It's an excellent example of a brand message. It explains the overarching purpose that drives all the work they do at every level of the organization. The founder and CEO has created a culture built around hospitality and tells a compelling brand story about that culture.

The company lives out their brand story in the way they treat subcontractors, who they prefer to call "trade partners." After all, once construction on a project is complete, they might not see the client for years. But they interact with subcontractors over and over again, so the company sees real value in making sure those relationships are treated very highly.

Living out the culture is so important to them that they are the only contractor we know of with a full-time "culture leader" on staff. They take the utmost care of their people, create true partnerships with subcontractors, and practice transparency with clients to a degree that is practically unheard of in the industry. They're determined to deliver a five-star service that makes people feel truly valued and appreciated—the essence of hospitality.

It's imperative that you tie your company, your brand, and the work done by every employee into some purpose, some brand story, that inspires. How are you making a difference in the lives of customers, or employees, or your community, or the world? That's what people want to know. And when you can articulate it clearly, people will connect more deeply, work harder, and stay longer.

Now, when a coaching staff takes over a struggling sports program with a long-term goal of winning a national championship, it's not enough to have an inspiring purpose. Most teams have an inspiring vision for the success they wish to achieve. You also need great playbooks, and every team member must be highly trained and highly effective at executing the plays correctly every time.

THE PURPOSE PRINCIPLE: ACTIONS TO TAKE

- A high-level, aspirational, inspirational "Just Cause" for your company can become a powerful tool for communicating purpose to every employee and serve as the North Star for every decision you make going forward.

- Figure out how your company is going to strategize differently. If you follow the same strategy as everyone else in your industry, how are people going to notice you?

- When you're crystal clear about who you are, what you stand for, and where you're going, then decision-making becomes so much easier. Transform this into a brand story that will land strongly with your target audience.

- It's imperative that you tie your company, your brand, and the work done by every employee into some purpose, some brand story, that inspires. Young people today demand meaningful work. They want to feel like they're doing something that matters.

PRINCIPLE THREE

PLAYBOOKS

"Every system is perfectly designed to get the results it gets."

—W. EDWARDS DEMING

If your company made $12 million last year at 4 percent net profit, then you have a system that is perfectly designed to deliver $12 million at 4 net percent profit. If you want better results, you're going to have to design a better system. However, when your processes exist only as tribal knowledge in the mind of the owner or other key people, then it is very difficult to understand and analyze your system as a whole, which makes it difficult to discover and implement changes that will allow you to scale.

It's a situation that happens in a lot of small businesses. The founder creates a process that works well, but it only exists in her head. When she brings in new people, she shares that process verbally, but since it's not captured in some kind of documentation, it is harder to teach the process to others as the business grows. Eventually, growth stalls as best practices slip.

When there's only one person on the team who knows how to do payroll, or how to operate some piece of machinery, or how to do the programming, then you've created a single point of failure. If you lose that person, if they're sick or on vacation, then no one can pass on the tribal knowledge about that area of the company. In some cases, the work they do comes to a complete stop until they return. No one does payroll for two weeks. No one operates that particular piece of machinery. And if that person leaves the company for good, then you're in real trouble.

Sometimes this tribal knowledge isn't documented for malicious reasons. The person who possesses it thinks, "If I don't write down what I know about this process, then the company can't get rid of me, because I'm the only one who knows how to do it." We've heard those exact words from people more than once. Essentially, one person is holding the company hostage as a means to job security.

It might protect that one person's job, but it also prevents the company from growing beyond a certain point. To overcome this limiting factor, you need to document your processes, create best practices, and train your employees to a high standard of excellence in carrying them out. This is absolutely vital if you want a business that is repeatable and scalable.

DOCUMENTING TRIBAL KNOWLEDGE

This is where your playbooks come into play. The fact is most businesses remain small and can't scale. Chances are, within a few miles of your home, there are hundreds, if not thousands, of businesses that have been around for years but never figured out how to grow. Mechanics, bookkeepers, tax preparers, dentists—these solopreneurs have never documented their processes in a way that would make their businesses scalable and repeatable.

What they do, and how they do it, has never been transformed into a system that others can easily follow. All that information exists solely in the mind of one person.

Why would an entrepreneur pay over a million dollars to own a McDonald's franchise? Certainly not because they want to learn how to cook hamburgers. Most of the time, it's because they want to learn how to operate a business with a proven system that will produce 18 percent to the bottom line. They invest heavily upfront so they can go to Hamburger University in Chicago and learn the McDonald's systems because it delivers consistent results, and that's a lot more reliable than trying to build your own fast-food restaurant from the ground up.

If you're ever going to grow, you have to take the "tribal knowledge" in your business and transform it into well-documented systems and checklists that people can use over and over again to deliver predictable outcomes for your customers or clients.

CHAPTER SEVEN

DOCUMENTING YOUR PROCESSES

You need to document your processes in a way that makes it easy to train your people, so they operate in the best possible way. All of the clients who have gone through this process with our guides have said afterward that they learned things about their own business functions that they hadn't realized before. There's something about working through and documenting your processes that clarifies them for you and reveals best practices.

In football, each team has a playbook full of plays that they've practiced over and over again, so they can execute them at the right time during a game. For each play, the specific actions of each player and position are spelled out, so everyone knows what they're supposed to do.

Even the best professional NFL players need playbooks. Otherwise, you wind up with suboptimal performance, which can turn to chaos on the field. A mediocre college team with good playbooks could probably beat an NFL team without playbooks. That's how important they are to performance.

It's exactly the same in your organization. So, how exactly do you transform tribal knowledge into documented processes that others can follow?

PROCESS OPTIMIZER

Before Michael became a business guide, in his previous career running a manufacturing company, he once brought in a Lean expert to help systemize the workflow processes inside the operational component of the business. Indeed, from very early in his career, Michael has been a big fan of applying Lean methodologies and using expert facilitators and consultants to guide him and his team.

When he later transitioned into working as a business guide, he came to realize that the majority of the issues that organizations face are either process or people problems. Often, there's a lack of performance because the company doesn't offer people the right training. Leaders haven't given them the right tools and resources—the right *playbooks*—to be successful.

When Michael first began working as a business guide, he would often share with his clients his belief that most problems in an organization are due to either having the wrong people or to a lack or processes. Almost every client agreed with him. He would then suggest that without clearly defined and optimized processes and training in place, it would be difficult to accurately determine if they had a "people" issue, as they might not be providing them a key resource they need in order to be successful.

Again, his clients agreed. However, when he encouraged them to create playbooks to help their people perform better, clients almost always procrastinated. They were either too busy to follow through on documenting their playbooks or they didn't have anyone in leadership to champion the idea and take the lead, resulting in them creating mediocre playbooks at best, if they even got around to creating them at all.

Frustrated, Michael decided to provide the solution himself, so he partnered with Lean expert and former P.F. Chang's Executive Vice-President, Heidi Berger, and created a company called Process Optimizer®.[11] Let's take a look at how it works.

Process Optimizer utilizes a team of trained facilitators, all Lean certified, to work with companies to document and optimize their processes in just nine days, instead of the nine months to nine years it takes most organizations to do on their own. When a company goes through the process of getting their playbooks documented, Process Optimizer takes a look at the organization from start to finish: from marketing and generating leads, to converting leads to customers or clients, to operations making or delivering products and services, to finance and administration managing the money and reporting.

For each of these major functions, there needs to be a playbook that documents the process in a way that makes it trainable. Process Optimizer works with teams throughout the organiza-

---

11   Visit www.ProcessOptimizer.Biz to learn more.

tions they assist to identify 1) what triggers each process to start, 2) what the desired outcome looks like, 3) what the subsequent steps are and in what specific order, and 4) what the timeline and handoff looks like.

For example, let's suppose you're documenting an operations process. It's triggered by an order being signed by the sales team. Once the sales team hands off an assigned order to the operations team, that triggers the first step in the ops process. These things should be clearly identified in your playbook.

Then the company needs to think through each of the steps that follow. What is the very next thing that operations should do once they've received an order from sales? Additionally, what are some things that improve the handoff? What are possible sources of friction that should be avoided or improved? Figure this out for each step of the process until there's a handoff to another team or another segment of the organization.

At Pinnacle, we either guide our clients through this process, or help them bring in an outside resource to do it for them. We believe every organization is perfectly capable of creating good playbooks on their own. You already have the tribal knowledge. You just have to capture it in a document that can be used to train others.

Our Pinnacle Business Guides often recommend Process Optimizer to do this work, and in the end, whether you do it yourself or get help, the goal is to create documented playbooks for each of your processes that anyone can use for training purposes. A good playbook should include checklists that need to be followed, as well as quick and easy references to make sure that no one misses a step.

We recommend that even frontline employees participate in creating playbooks. If you want to get employees to buy in, then you have to give them an opportunity to weigh in. Make sure their voices are heard as you analyze and document each step in your operational processes. If you only use leaders and a few direct reports to do this, you're likely to miss out on some vital components in the flow of your processes. Even frontline employees can offer important suggestions for optimizing processes.

Once you have a playbook, then you have a powerful resource for identifying the source of your problems. Let's suppose you have a week where you don't get the results you were looking for. A package doesn't get delivered on time, and now a customer is frustrated. To figure out where you went wrong, you can go back to the playbook to make sure you didn't miss a step somewhere along the way.

"Oh, we were supposed to call the customer at this point to make sure they knew the delivery would be late." In that case, you know you need a bit more training on that step.

Or perhaps you realize that you need to add a step to the process. "The playbook doesn't say that someone is supposed to call the customer at this step. It wasn't the employee's fault." Now, you've identified another place where you can optimize your process. Either way, having a playbook makes it much easier to figure out why you're not getting the results you anticipated, so you know where to focus your efforts for improvement.

Remember, as we said, most performance problems are either a result of a lack of processes or having the wrong people in the business, so being able to quickly and accurately determine which one it is makes a world of difference. When there's a problem, you simply ask the question, "Do we have something in our playbook that would have prevented this?"

If the answer is yes, then you know it's a people issue, and you can train them. Or, if they can't do the job even with training, you put someone in the seat who can. If the answer is no, then you can add or improve a step in the playbook, both adding the step *and* making sure you let everyone who runs that play know that the process has been updated and the step has been added. We recommend that you assign a champion to own each specific playbook, and if it needs updating, they are empowered to update the playbook and make it a living document.

OVERCOMMUNICATE

The best-run companies communicate and overcommunicate their playbooks. When your processes are simplified and documented, then you can spend your time and energy creating an exceptional experience for employees and customers rather than spending all of your time just trying to deliver your service, get the work done, or get an order out of the door.

At Pinnacle, when we interview clients, we always ask about their playbooks. Greg recently interviewed a sales manager with twenty years of experience, and he asked him if he had a sales management playbook. After all, with twenty years of experience, he has surely developed some tribal knowledge about how to do sales management well. He must have a few best practices stored in his brain somewhere, but had he ever taken that tribal knowledge and written it down in a way that others could follow?

When Greg asked him about his playbook, he replied, "What do you mean? What would be in the playbook?"

That kind of response is typical. So, Greg explained it to him: "Using all of your experience, you should be able to create a sales management playbook that tells people how you recruit salespeople and onboard them. It should provide some examples of contests you can use to drive sales, as well as your idea of an effective sales process. What do you do if you lose a salesperson? How do you communicate it, and how do you make sure clients are not impacted? Everything from beginning to end should be documented in a way that is simple, trainable, and scalable so that the organization has a true 'sales machine.'"

In the end, Greg didn't hire the sales manager. The applicant may have had twenty years of experience, but in reality, he was doing the same thing he did when he first started in the business twenty years earlier—keeping everything in his head and never documenting anything. You could argue the applicant had one year of experience and twenty years of practice.

If you interviewed a sales manager who brought in their "sales playbook" that told you exactly how they recruit, onboard, manage, compensate, train, and hold salespeople accountable, and it looked like they were very serious about their career, you would get up and lock the interview room door and not let that person leave because of the value they brought to the position. Sadly, when it comes to hiring for leaderships positions, most applicants don't bring their playbooks.

Playbooks are so incredibly important, yet they are so very rare, especially in small businesses. Remember, when someone buys a franchise, they're actually buying that company's playbook. Whether or not you intend to franchise your business in the future, we encourage you to build a franchise-able business by creating playbooks that make your vision and business model easier to grow and scale.

And if you already have a playbook, ask yourself this, "How much would somebody pay for it?" What kind of franchise fee could your business command? If your playbook is a dusty box of files in a corner somewhere, or a file tucked in the Z drive on your computer network with fifty different versions, then it's probably not worth much, if anything.

If someone wanted to buy your business outright, would your existing playbook increase or decrease the value? Or would it tank the sale altogether? If there are certain people within your organization who have golden handcuffs because you can't afford to lose their tribal knowledge, then your playbooks need more work. Remember, your goal is to document all of your processes thoroughly from beginning to end, identifying best practices and things to avoid, in a way that is both scalable and trainable.

Let's look at some best practices for getting the most out of your playbooks.

CHAPTER EIGHT

PRACTICE SCHEDULES

You can't simply hand a playbook to a team member and expect them to learn it on their own. You must show them the playbook in action, demonstrate what high performance looks like, and then practice *with* them.

You can't just send a new employee to the frontlines and expect them to perform at a high level. Every employee needs a playbook and practice schedule to ensure that they know what they're supposed to do at every step of every process. Even when they've been with you for a while, they need time to go "offstage" and practice the basics, or they'll start slipping over time.

As Admiral Hyman Rickover, the "Father of the Nuclear Navy," put it, "Good ideas are not adopted automatically. They must be driven into practice with courageous impatience."[12]

---

12 Hyman Rickover, "Doing a Job," speech, 1982, Columbia University, transcript, https://govleaders.org/rickover.htm.

SPEND MORE TIME PRACTICING

Most sports teams practice more than they play. NFL players spend a lot more time on the practice field than in actual games. Professional golfers go to the driving range numerous times and play many rounds of practice golf before they play in a tournament. And, for the most part, this practice isn't done sporadically. Athletes follow practice schedules.

This isn't limited to sports. Teachers don't just walk into the classroom and start teaching off the top of their heads. Rather, they spend a lot of time creating lesson plans long before they ever speak to a single student. When a trial lawyer has a big case, they don't just walk into the courtroom and start talking. They spend many hours preparing the case, and then they practice, practice, and practice some more. By the time they get into the courtroom, they know every question they're going to ask, and they've thought through every answer they might get.

Before a surgeon performs surgery, they talk through the procedure at length with their team and work out all the steps they're going to take. Before musicians take the stage, they practice their songs for many hours. Even after they practice, before taking the stage, they still do a sound check.

In so many fields, people spend far more time practicing and getting ready than they do performing their actual job. Yet somehow, in the business world, we don't spend nearly enough time getting our people to practice. We just send them to the frontlines and hope for the best.

The companies that get this right really stand out.

Greg's daughter Samantha worked for Chick-fil-A, and he was very impressed with just how much time they spend preparing their people. In fact, Chick-fil-A says they aren't primarily a restaurant or food service company; they're a training and development company. If you've been to one of their locations, you've experienced firsthand their commitment to excellence.

This focus on training and development has contributed to their success more than anything else. It's the reason why a fast-food business with a very limited menu that is closed on Sundays has a far more zealous following than much bigger chains like McDonald's and Starbucks. The real power comes from practicing their playbooks constantly. That's how Chick-fil-A maintains such a high standard throughout the customer's experience.

CHAPTER NINE

MEETING STRUCTURES

If you've ever worked with a Business Operating System, then you know most of them have weekly meetings that tend to follow a very specific, predetermined agenda. Consequently, if you try to bring up things that aren't on the agenda, things that you feel are missing, your coach is almost always going to take you back to the book.

"This is the *pure* way to do it. This is how it's done, so you need to do it this way."

One of our clients recently recounted their own experiences in a popular Business Operating System. They kept trying to deviate from the weekly meeting agenda because they were frustrated about some aspects of the meeting and the system that weren't working for them. Finally, their coach said, "If the weekly meeting isn't working for you, maybe *you're* the problem. Maybe it's *you* that's not working." This lack of flexibility and "one-size-fits-all" thinking eventually drove them away from the Business Operating System, and they're now working with Pinnacle.

In the business world, meetings are how we communicate, make decisions, and get alignment. They're incredibly important, but they can also be a sore point, especially when the agenda is not conducive to the intent of the meeting. To that end, at Pinnacle, we recommend a few different types of meetings to fit a variety of purposes, and we always work with our clients to customize those meetings to get the most value for them based on their unique needs.

THE DAILY STAND-UP

The idea for the "Daily Stand-Up" came from Horst Schulze, president and COO of Ritz-Carlton Company. As Senior VP Leonardo Inghilleri explained, "We tell our employees to move heaven and earth to satisfy a customer. We have to equip them to do that—every day."[13]

The purpose of this daily meeting, he says, is, "Part training, part operations, part philosophy—all conducted with drill-like efficiency." Put another way, the goal is to 1) **keep team members aligned and connected**, and 2) **execute faster with a game plan for the day and/or shift**. It's called a "Stand-Up" because it works best when everyone remains standing. That keeps it quick and efficient.

The agenda for the meeting should cover three things:

- What happened yesterday that the team needs to know?
- What is happening today that the team needs to know?
- Where do you need help? Where are you stuck?

---

13 Cathy Olofson, "The Ritz Puts on Stand-Up Meetings," *Fast Company*, August 31, 1998, https://www.fastcompany.com/35474/ritz-puts-stand-meetings.

The Daily Stand-Up is ideally ten to fifteen minutes, has a cool name, and starts at an odd time. For example, at Pinnacle, we call them "Daily Beats," and they start at 8:08 a.m. We know of a medical technology company whose work consists largely of asking people to swish and spit into a test tube so they can check for antibodies. They call their Daily Stand-Up "Spit It Out," which we thought was quite clever.

If you have a remote team, a Daily Stand-Up is a great opportunity to get them on a call and find out what's happening in their world that day (or the day before). You can learn what people are struggling with, make sure everyone is on the same page, and touch base on pressing issues.

THE WEEKLY TACTICAL

A second type of meeting is called "The Weekly Tactical," and it's all about priorities, debates, and execution. The purpose is to keep everyone informed about what's going on and ensure projects are moving forward. To do that, you need to 1) **check in on important numbers** (aka, "Did we win the week?"), 2) **ensure that quarterly priorities stay top of mind**, and 3) **keep a pulse on your team and customers.**

This meeting should be around ninety minutes for the leadership team. We suggest bringing a list of items that need to be addressed, but also giving your people a chance to share how they're doing and what they're dealing with. Review metrics, share project updates, and facilitate discussion. The agenda might look something like this:

- Set the stage—The first ten minutes is a hook for the rest of the meeting, so own the stage.
- Check-In—"What's up?"
- Scoreboard—"Did we win the week? If so, why, or why not?"
- FAST Rock Review—"Tell us in one sentence…"
  - "What did you do last week to move this forward?"
  - "What will you do this week to continue to move this forward?"
- Accountability from last week—"Did you do what you promised to do from last week?"
- Team Engagement—"What did you do this week that was a magical moment for a direct report or team member?"
- Business Development/Voice of the Customer—brief headlines on business development and the voice of the customer. We believe a leadership team should be talking about growing the business and taking care of customers at a high level.
- The List of Topics—Everything you need this team to hear or help with. Decisions to make, information to share, need help, or obstacles to tackle.
- Wrap Up Aligned
  - "Who needs to know what?"
  - "Summarize the priorities for this week."
  - "Did we have enough healthy conflict and debate? Yes/No"
  - "Did we have a great meeting? Rating 1-6"

MONTHLY FINANCIAL REVIEW

Finally, there's real value in having a Monthly Financial Review with leaders so each leader grows in their understanding of the financial realities of your organization. Take one of your weekly Tactical Meetings and use this agenda instead. Your goals are to 1) **improve financial health** and 2) **get your leadership team to**

own ALL quarterly numbers and understand where they are and what they need to do.

At a bare minimum, you should review your income statement, budget variance, financial forecast, and accounts receivable payments. Each member of the leadership team who has a Rock, brings their FAST Rock planner and the work they have done to show the team how they are progressing with rocks. This creates transparency and greater accountability. Waiting until the deadline to review rocks doesn't usually end well. We are all about "trust but verify." The leadership team owns all the company quarterly FAST Rocks, so make sure they are not only doing them but doing them *well*.

Your agenda might look something like this:

- Catch Up
  - Ask a thought-provoking question.
  - "Any uh-oh moments this month?"
- Review Prior Month Financials:
  - Actual vs. budget variance report (deep dive into deviations with your general ledger if needed)
  - Balance sheet
  - Thirteen-week cash flow
- Leadership team members bring their FAST Rock Planner and Rock details to show the leadership team exactly where they are in their progress with completing their FAST Rock and discussing what's next to keep them on track.
- One or two big topics—These topics should improve your financial position, get numbers back on track, or get the FAST Rock back on track.
- Action items

- Wrap up aligned

MAKE EVERY MEETING MATTER

We have ten essential meeting frameworks in Pinnacle. The Daily Stand-Up, the Weekly Tactical, and the Monthly Financial Review are just three examples of the kinds of meetings we typically recommend to clients. You can also conduct a quarterly "State of the Company" meeting (or, as we like to call it, the "State of the Climb"), which is an all-hands meeting that keeps everyone informed about where the organization is going, how we're going to get there, and how we're performing.

The point of this section is not to go through every possible type of meeting. Rather, we're suggesting that when you conduct meetings in your business, you need to make sure that you provide real value. Love them; own them. It's your stage. If people are on their phones, distracted, rambling, then they clearly don't see the value in the meeting. While you should definitely call out the distractions, the deeper issue is to work to understand why the meeting lacks value for some of the attendees and work to fix that. It could be the agenda items, or it could be that some team members don't really need to be in the meeting.

It's up to the meeting leader to change the agenda to make it more meaningful and engaging. Try starting with an amusing video or reading a headline—whatever you need to do. Meetings don't have to suck! Take ownership of the meeting and make it valuable.

In the Business Operating System world, it is not uncommon during weekly meetings for team members to give an update on their quarterly priorities (Rocks) by stating they are "on track" to achieve their priority or that they are "off track." This portion of the weekly meetings often amounted to a string of team members saying, "On track. On track. On track." What is missing are specifics that help the team with accountability.

Where we have encountered this with clients moving to Pinnacle, we invigorate these meetings with a change in expectations. Instead of a mere confirmation of progress toward quarterly priorities, we encouraged team members to share specific actions they'd taken that week to advance their priorities (FAST Rocks). For example, when reviewing FAST Rocks, a team member might say, "I posted the ad, conducted three interviews, and successfully invited two candidates for a second interview. My next step is to update the ad this week." This approach breathed new life into their meetings, transforming them from monotonous check-ins into engaging and productive sessions.

Take ownership of your meetings! Give them a fun name, give them structure, include an agenda that considers the specific needs of your attendees, and above all, make sure people are engaged. If it's a meeting with clients or prospects, consider the experience they'll have when they arrive. Is your facility inviting? Is their name on the board? Is the room full of energy? Have you provided beverages and scratch pads with pens and paper? Is the temperature comfortable?

Again, this is your stage, and as the meeting leader, you're like any other performer on stage. Make it a compelling performance that draws attendees in.

Meetings are how you get work done, how decisions are made, and how you get alignment, weigh-in, and buy-in. It is imperative that you make sure they're a good use of your time. You should have a playbook for conducting these meetings that tells you how they will unfold, how you will engage people, and how you will make sure that the most important topics get covered.

Once your playbooks are in order, you can begin holding people to a higher standard of performance, because great playbooks make it easier for your A-players to achieve their best. A good coach knows they can expect more from their team when they have provided their players with well-designed playbooks. Why? Because all the relevant plays are contained in that book. Every player in every position knows what is expected of them, how best to achieve it, and how their role interacts with every other player. Furthermore, they've studied and practiced that playbook like crazy.

So, with that in mind, let's look at how you can create an environment where your people can perform at their very best.

THE PLAYBOOK PRINCIPLE: ACTIONS TO TAKE

- Document your processes, create best practices, and train your employees to a certain standard of excellence in carrying them out. This is vital if you want a business that is repeatable and scalable.

- You can't simply hand a playbook to a team member and expect them to learn it on their own. You have to show them the playbook in action and then practice with them.

- Make sure your meetings provide real value. Give them a fun name, give them structure, include an agenda that considers the specific needs of your attendees, and above all, make sure people are engaged.

- When your processes are simplified and documented, then you can spend your time and energy creating an exceptional experience for employees and customers.

PRINCIPLE FOUR

PERFORMANCE

"With your A-game, you can beat anybody; anything less, and they can beat you."

—NICK SABAN

You'll never be an elite wealth manager, hockey player, or salesperson if you're not obsessed with getting to a high level. Remember, passion can be lost. And what happens when a person loses their passion for what they're doing? Then it becomes "just a job," or a grind, or they stop doing it altogether.

But having passion isn't enough by itself. You need expert guidance to improve and achieve your best. Even the greatest players in the world have coaches. In his prime, Tiger Woods had three coaches: one for his long game, one for his short game, and then a sports psychologist for his mental game. Every player needs a great leader who sets clear expectations and helps them meet those expectations.

Nick Saban is considered one of the greatest football coaches in college football history. He's won seven national championship titles, and he was the first college football coach to win a national championship with two different NCAA schools. He has coached the University of Alabama since 2007, but he formerly coached the Miami Dolphins, LSU, Michigan State, and the University of Toledo.

In a short video that is readily available on YouTube, Saban quotes Freddie Kitchens, who took over as head coach of the Cleveland Browns in 2019. According to Nick, Freddie said:

> We have about five choices in our life. We can be *bad* at what we do. We can be *average* at what we do. We can be *good* at what we do, which is probably God's expectation for whatever ability He gave us. Or we can be *excellent*. Or we can be *elite*. And everybody has a choice as to what they want to do and how they want to do it. But if you're going to be excellent or elite, you've got to do special things. You have to have special intensity. You have to have special focus. You have to have a special commitment, drive, and passion to do things at a high level and a high standard all the time. And it doesn't matter what God-given ability you have, that probably can make you good, but without the rest of it, I'm not sure you ever get excellent or elite.[14]

This quote is something that business leaders need to think about. What are you doing to become excellent or elite at what

---

14 McDonnell Consulting Group, "Sandler Training Tips: Nick Saban – McDonell Consulting Group, Sandler Training," YouTube video, 0:59, https://www.youtube.com/watch?v=u1BvMoAqWog.

you do? Or have you settled for just being "good"? At Pinnacle, we're always working with our clients to help them become a category of one in the markets they serve, and you can't do that if you're not fiercely driven to be excellent or elite.

Some companies have that drive internally; others need outside coaching to get there. But it all comes down to having a real passion for what you do. This isn't limited to sports or the business world, by any means. If you want to be excellent or elite at *anything* in life, what do you do? Read books, do research, study, get some coaching, learn, and practice hard! If you're not passionate, then you're probably not going to do all of that.

CHAPTER TEN

SCOREBOARDS

Pick any professional sport, and you'll find that there are stats that players track because they want to know—they *need* to know—how they're doing at all times. This is always the case when you're passionate about your performance. You *want* to be measured because you *want* to be the absolute best you can be.

Every professional athlete knows how many wins and losses they've had, how many home runs they've hit, their free throw percentage. They know their batting average, their number of offensive yards per carry, their average number of shots on goal.

In hockey, there's a stat called the "plus-minus rating." A player is awarded a "plus" every time they're on the ice when a goal is scored by their team, and they receive a "minus" every time they are on the ice when a goal is scored by the opposing team. A higher plus-minus rating suggests that a player has an influential role in the game, so of course, every hockey player knows their rating. It may go up or down over time, but every player knows where it is and how they're doing at the moment.

It's not just the players who care about the numbers. Fans follow them as well. During any broadcast of a professional sporting game, a portion of the screen is plastered with numbers that tell viewers exactly where they are in the game and how it's going. Often, individual players are highlighted with special graphics that reveal their performance stats.

Can you imagine what it would be like if broadcasters didn't provide this information? What if there was no scoreboard? Would anyone watch a football game if no one kept score and no player or game stats were tracked?

It's not all that different in the business world. Every single team member in your organization wants to know, and needs to know, the score at all times. In fact, we believe that at the root of all performance problems, there's usually a lack of clear expectations and no scoreboard. When people don't know what's expected of them and can't measure how they're doing, then they're not going to be motivated to reach farther, try harder, or do more.

STATS CREATE EXPECTATIONS

Are there some athletes who don't track their stats? Are there some games where there is no scoreboard? Certainly. When a group of people decide to shoot hoops at the local park, they don't have a scoreboard, it doesn't really matter who wins and who loses, and as a result, they are likely only going to give their best efforts for brief moments, if at all. However, when they are keeping score, you can tell they are keeping score from across the field just by observing their body language.

If your company is not keeping score, then it's only practice.

Player stats create expectations that encourage great performance. If you're a serious hockey player and you see your plus-minus rating fall, you're going to be at the rink forty-five minutes earlier so you can work on your game. And if you have good playbooks as a reference, you can figure out exactly what you need to work on with that extra practice time.

When Michael lived in North Carolina and Virginia, he was deeply involved as a booster and committee member in the athletics program at UNC-Chapel Hill. During that time, he had the opportunity to meet and get to know Hall of Famer and longtime head coach Roy Williams. Roy once told Michael a story about his time as an assistant coach at UNC and an experience with J. R. Reid, who was a star player on the Carolina men's basketball team from 1986 to 1989. As Roy explained, J. R. Reid wasn't a particularly good free-throw shooter, so opposing teams would intentionally get him fouled late in the game.

Ultimately, Reid became a bit of a liability because of this. Now, he was a good player in other ways and got a lot of points on the scoreboard during regular play. Plus, at six-foot-nine, his sheer size was an advantage. Many coaches would have simply tolerated his poor free-throw performance. However, Head Coach Dean Smith and the coaching staff were determined to do something about it, so they frequently made Reid stay after practice and shoot a hundred free throws non-stop while an assistant coach sat on a stool nearby and talked to him about his form.

This wasn't intended as some strange form of punishment. Rather, they were investing time in helping him develop his free-throw form and technique so he could achieve his best.

This approach translates well to our organizations. When people aren't hitting their numbers or meeting their metrics, we should neither tolerate their excuses and accept mediocrity nor simply chastise them. Rather, as leaders, we need to work with them to develop and improve their skills.

That's how you create a culture of performance. Practice doesn't make perfect. Rather, *perfect* practice makes perfect. The Carolina coaching staff didn't just put J. R. Reid at the free-throw line and say, "Go for it." An assistant coach was there to provide guidance and correction. It's this way in any sport. If you have a bad hook in your golf swing, the best way to improve it is to practice your golf swing a thousand times *and* get professional help with your swing.

In other words, give your people the numbers they need in order to track their own performance, and then provide the guidance they need to bring those numbers up. These two things are absolutely essential if you want to create a high-performing culture!

WRESTLE VICTORY FROM THE JAWS OF DEFEAT

Earlier, we mentioned our HVAC client. The company began tracking return trips, which they called RTFs, or "Returns to Finish," and they were alarmed at just how often they happened. Approximately 49 percent of their service calls each day resulted in the need to return for a second trip to finish the service call because they were missing parts or dispatched the wrong tech to the job.

At our Annual Summit a couple years ago, Greg was taking the leadership team through an exercise to discover the company's

"One Phrase" strategy that could be used to drive the economic engine of the business, improve client experience, employee morale, and bottom-line profitability. The visionary of the company came up with the catchphrase "One Trip™," which he has since trademarked. The idea was to solve the problem that almost 50 percent of the time it took two service calls to fix a client's issue. So, the first thing we did was create a scoreboard for the week, where we could track things like average daily invoices, productivity per team member, and revenue per trip. Most importantly, we tracked those "Return to Finish" appointments so the company could gauge which activities lowered the daily number.

The company fully embraced this approach. To this day, you could walk into the company, or hop on the phone with the leadership team, and ask, "How are we doing today?" And everyone would know. They would know today's goals and whether or not the team is going to win the day based on the data.

The company has been around for seventy-five years, and they always had financials and performance reviews, but for most of their history, they got the numbers too late to impact current performance. This is a common problem. First, you must close out the month. Then you must wait two or three weeks for a bookkeeper to get you the numbers. By the time you see them, they're six or seven weeks old, which makes it hard to use them to change behavior.

No sport has a scoreboard that is six or seven weeks behind. On the contrary, score is kept up to the minute. You can look up and see where you are in the game, who's winning or losing, how much time is left, and more. Beyond that, the coaches on the sidelines have all kinds of data they can use to make leadership decisions on the fly.

When there are twelve seconds left on the clock and the score is close, the whole tenor of the game changes. Everyone becomes more focused and intense. The crowd goes wild as coaches and players work furiously to wrestle victory from the jaws of defeat until the last possible moment.

When a company has an up-to-the-minute scoreboard, every team member knows how they're doing at any particular moment. If they see that the day is almost over and they haven't quite won their numbers, they can rally, intensify their efforts, and try to pull out a last-minute victory.

Sadly, few companies operate like this. Walk into any company, go to operations, or dispatch, or any other team, and ask them for their numbers. They'll probably give you a vague answer like, "We're on time," but they won't have specific up-to-the-minute numbers that reveal exactly how they're doing and whether or not they're on track to win the day.

Notice we're recommending "scoreboards," not "scorecards." Quite frankly, scorecards tend to wind up sitting in the Z drive somewhere under a password key. A scoreboard, on the other hand, is a living thing, always accessible and providing the most current numbers so you always know how everyone is doing.

Here's an example of what a business scoreboard might look like.

WIN THE WEEK FOR PRODUCTION LINE ONE

	WHAT NEEDS TO GET DONE	WHAT WE DID	X	✓
MON	2,633 ft	2,703 ft		●
TUE	2,859 ft	2,843 ft	●	
WED	2,622 ft	2,648 ft		●
THU	2,509 ft	2,515 ft		●
FRI	2,822 ft	2,817 ft	●	
TOTAL	13,445 ft	13,526 ft	WON	

RED LIGHT/GREEN LIGHT

During Michael's time as Owner and CEO of Erath Veneer, he and his leadership team spent a tremendous amount of time and effort discovering and analyzing their "profit per X," which in this case meant "gross profit dollars per board foot produced." The more they could do to maximize gross profit dollars per board foot produced, the better they would perform financially. The company's biggest constraint was throughput (the amount of material passing through production lines in a given period of time).

Since they were already operating on two and a half shifts, they couldn't expand production without adding new machinery and production lines, which would have cost several million dollars per additional line. This was cost prohibitive and their biggest internal choke point, so they had to find another way to grow EBITDA[15] once they reached that production capacity ceiling.

As CEO, Michael needed to deliver consistent growth in enterprise value. Before the company reached their sales and production capacity ceilings, this was only a matter of growing sales and increasing production, but once the choke point was reached, they had to be more strategic in order to grow their "profit per X."

They looked for a way to communicate to employees how they were doing against productivity goals and incentivize them to be more efficient, while at the same time, protecting the quality of the product. The solution they came up with was to give employees a scoreboard and live communication system.

They set goals each day for each shift and production line about what their total board footage per shift needed to be. Then, every morning, they would print a color bar graph showing the past five days of production by day, shift, and production line, and they taped it to the break room door where every employee would see it when they went on break. This way, every employee could see exactly how their team, and the overall production department, was performing.

Implementing this daily scoreboard, even without any additional financial incentives, caused an increase in productivity, because no one wanted to be on a team that was consistently in the red. This began generating awareness and drove a sense of competition, as teams began challenging each other to become more productive.

---

15   Earnings before interest, taxes, depreciation, and amortization.

At the same time, the company implemented a system to protect quality. They set up their machines with a limit switch so that, at a certain point in the production or slicing of a log, the limit switch would turn on a light, indicating to the operator that it was time to pull a single sheet of veneer as a sample. He or she would mark the time of day and log number on the sample sheet with a wax crayon, as well as which production line and shift it came from. All the samples were saved, and the following morning, before creating that day's bar graph, Michael's COO and their production manager would check each sample for defects using a light table and a micrometer.

If any samples failed to meet quality criteria, they were set aside, and the board footage from that log was deducted from the team's total for the prior day before the bar graph was produced. This created a mindset where the operators of the machines, who had control over both productivity and quality, constantly tried to balance efficiency with product quality. They didn't want to spend time producing veneer that wouldn't contribute to their daily goal.

After a few weeks of doing this, Michael and his team realized that while very helpful, the bar graph scoreboards were still a slightly lagging indicator, so one of the veneer slicer operators came up with a suggestion during a daily huddle. He asked if there was a way to add a light by the machine that he could turn on when he was falling behind, to signal to others that there was a problem. Michael ran with the idea, and within a few days, he had tower lights (red, yellow, green vertical lights) installed at every production line. The lights were tied to a simple toggle switch that the machine operator could position.

At the start of each shift, all lights would be green. As the day progressed, operators tracked their individual productivity on a per-hour basis, and if they fell below their rate for the day, they flipped the switch to red. Anybody walking through the factory, from a supervisor, manager, salesperson, or even Michael, who saw a red light would immediately go to that machine and see what they could do to help get things back on track. If an operator detected a potential maintenance issue, like a bearing that started making noise or the waste conveyor getting too full, they would turn the light yellow and a supervisor would immediately send a maintenance team member.

The whole production department became more efficient, which resulted in additional profit being made, simply by providing a tool that helped the production team become more informed, more efficient, and more engaged. When those efficiency gains were coupled with a focus on pricing strategy and raw materials cost management, the company as a whole became significantly more profitable and enterprise value increased dramatically.

But it was the power of those simple bar graph scoreboards and tower lights that made the real impact on productivity, because when people can see the score, they naturally play harder to win.

CHAPTER ELEVEN

THE POWER OF FLYWHEELS

A flywheel is a heavy, revolving wheel that increases a machine's momentum by storing rotational energy, which creates greater stability and smooths over any fluctuations. In his book *Good to Great*, Jim Collins explains how the flywheel concept can also be used to describe a company's business model.[16]

According to Collins, when a company goes through what he calls a "good to great transformation," it's never the result of a single innovation or some silver bullet. Rather, there are specific components of the business that drive growth as they gain momentum over time.

Collins describes it in this way, "Picture a huge, heavy flywheel—a massive metal disk mounted horizontally on an axle, about 30 feet in diameter, 2 feet thick, and weighing about 5,000 pounds. Now imagine that your task is to get the flywheel rotat-

---

16   Jim Collins, Good to Great: Why Some Companies Make the Leap and Others Don't (New York: Harper Collins, 2001).

ing on the axle as fast and long as possible."[17] That's what it's like trying to transform your business so it can grow and scale.

Here are two examples of company flywheels:

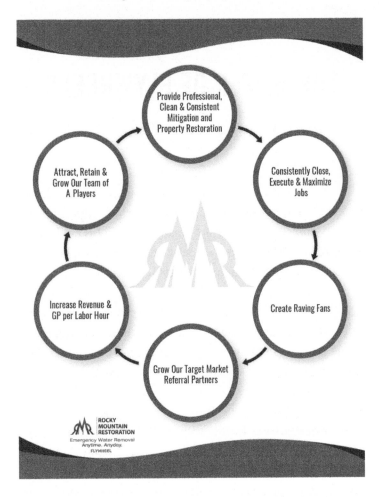

17   "The Flywheel Effect," JimCollins.com, accessed January 30, 2023, https://www.jimcollins.com/concepts/ the-flywheel.html.

The idea is that, by focusing on improving the individual components in a flywheel, a company accelerates growth over time. There's no single defining action or "miracle moment" that makes it happen. In the beginning, just like turning a giant, heavy flywheel, it takes great effort just to get it to inch forward. You keep pushing, and with persistent effort, eventually you get the flywheel to complete an entire turn.

However, you don't stop there. You keep pushing. Now, the flywheel moves a bit faster, and as it does, turning it becomes easier. As it builds more and more momentum, you find that it takes less effort to turn it. One rotation becomes two, then four, then eight.

At some point, you reach a breakthrough where the flywheel spins at a furious pace with almost unstoppable momentum.

As Collins explains, "Each turn of the flywheel builds upon work done earlier, compounding your investment of effort. A thousand times faster, then ten thousand, then a hundred thousand. The huge heavy disk flies forward, with almost unstoppable momentum."

It's the same for any company going through a transformation. Indeed, we see it with our own Pinnacle clients. When they first start working with a Pinnacle guide, it takes a lot of effort to start moving their company in a better direction, but if they apply consistent effort, it becomes easier and easier to continue to grow and scale and become a great business.

THE ELEMENTS OF YOUR FLYWHEEL

A company's flywheel is usually composed of five to seven elements, and getting them all in motion can be tough at first. But once they're in motion, it takes less and less effort to keep them going, as the flywheel gains momentum and turns faster and faster.

What are the components of a business flywheel? First, there's your *strategic differentiator*. This is how you provide consistent, differentiated value in the marketplace. Then there are various elements that tie into your strategy. These will vary depending on your industry.

To keep your flywheel gaining momentum, you need to get your executive team together on a quarterly basis to look at each of your components, so you can clearly see which teams in your organization make the greatest impact on turning the flywheel. Typically, we encourage leaders to ask each of their teams to evaluate how consistently they are performing well within each of these elements, using a rating scale of one to ten.

This will allow you to rank each of the components of your flywheel from strongest to weakest, so you can focus on the weaker components in the upcoming quarter. If you will do that consistently over time, you will gain momentum in producing results.

The flywheel concept makes it easier to communicate your business model to both employees and outsiders by connecting the dots between key components. It also makes it clear why your scoreboards matter, why it's important for each team member to hit their numbers, and why they should be obsessed with following your playbooks. Get the flywheel moving by strengthening each of the components, and growing and scaling your business will get easier over time.

CHAPTER TWELVE

COACHING CONVERSATIONS

What if you have some amazing high performer lurking in a low-level position in your company, someone who could turn the whole company around if given the chance? It's possible. We've seen it happen. It's up to you to find these people in your ranks and unlock their potential.

Sometimes, it's not a matter of being underappreciated. Some potential high performers are holding *themselves* back by not giving their best. All too often, leaders tolerate excuses that get in the way of performance. Sometimes, we have to push people to be their best. Having easy access to performance numbers through some kind of scoreboard helps you do that, but in the end, you have to create that culture of performance.

Most companies rely on annual performance reviews to keep employees on track, and most employees see them chiefly as an opportunity to get an annual raise. However, we find them to be largely ineffective. The time between these reviews is so long, who can really remember what the employee has done?

CONSTANT FEEDBACK

Everyone deserves to work for a great leader, and great leaders, in practice, operate like great coaches. A coach doesn't talk to his players once a year. He works with them continually and gives them constant feedback, including regular one-on-one conversations with individual players. Why? Because coaches want to get to know each player. They want to understand who they are, what motivates them, how they think and feel. They want to know what's working and what's not working, where each player feels like they are falling behind or excelling, what they need, and so on.

Employees need the same thing from their leaders. According to Gallup research on employee engagement, people want three things from their job: 1) They want a good relationship with their boss, 2) they want to know that their work matters, and 3) they want their job performance to be measured so there's no subjectivity to it.[18]

One way to ensure that you give your team all three is through *coaching conversations.*

You've seen it in sports at all levels. From time to time, the coach will pull a player to the sidelines and have a one-on-one conversation with them. It might be a tough conversation about their performance: "I need you to step up your game and start hitting those shots!" It might be a rallying cry: "We're down two points. You can do this. Get out there and get us that basket!" Or it might be praise: "I love how fast you're moving out there. Keep it up!"

---

18   "What Is Employee Engagement and How Do You Improve It?," Gallup, accessed January 30, 2023, https://www.gallup.com/workplace/285674/improve-employee-engagement-workplace.aspx.

Whatever the case, these coaching conversations are an opportunity to re-engage with players. You can do the same thing in your business. Have regular coaching conversations with individual team members. Are they falling behind? Pull them aside and see what's happening. Encourage them to get back on track and offer help. Do you see signs of stress in a particular person? Meet with them one-on-one and find out what's going on in their lives.

As Eric Schmidt, former CEO of Google, put it, "Everybody needs a coach." Even very successful business leaders have coaches. Bill Gates has a coach. Heck, even Warren Buffett has a coach. Her name is Sharon Osberg. Now, to be clear, she's Buffett's bridge coach. It turns out, Warren Buffett has a passion for playing bridge, and he found a world class player to improve his game. As Sharon has said about herself, "In photos of Bill [Gates] and Warren playing bridge, I am always the one whose back of the head is facing the camera."

She explains her coaching style in this way: "We would play in the evening, and I would go through teaching points. He absorbed it like a sponge."[19] You may not be teaching your people how to improve their bridge-playing skills, but you need to have regular coaching conversations with them so they can absorb your advice like a sponge.

A good coaching conversation looks for the positive while also addressing problem areas. People need both encouragement and correction. Many leaders only address people when there's a problem, so their coaching conversations come to be dreaded

---

19   Thomas Heath, "Meet the Woman Who Coaches Billionaires Warren Buffett and Bill Gates," *New Zealand Herald*, July 28, 2017, https://www.nzherald.co.nz/business/meet-the-woman-who-coaches-billionaires-warren-buffett-and-bill-gates/2TUSRCZJRLD26QXKG57DEHVDTU/.

by those reporting to them. Greg once worked for a boss (we'll call him "Marty") who was brutal. Marty operated by the motto, "There's always room for improvement," but he applied it without mercy.

Greg and his team could do ninety-nine things perfectly and one thing wrong, and Marty would only talk about the one thing they'd done wrong. It was relentless, and it shattered morale. You must get rid of a coach like that because people won't want to play for him. And indeed, the company finally parted ways with Marty and moved someone else into his position.

With the new leader, coaching conversations become encouraging and inspiring, while also corrective, and always with an eye toward helping people achieve their best. People loved him, and performance increased. They put scoreboards in place, so everyone knew exactly how they're doing. The performance culture became strong, and employees developed a great relationship with their new leader.

Don't underestimate the power of bringing in a great leader who is an effective coach. It's one of the most impactful hiring decisions you will ever make.

GETTING THE BEST FROM YOUR BEST

An A-player needs great coaching, great training, *and* ongoing encouragement. They have the potential, but it's up to you to fully unlock it. When you do that, they're going to do some amazing things for your company.

Michael Jordan was arguably the greatest basketball player of all time, but he needed the right team around him to really achieve his best. According to the documentary *The Last Dance*, Jordan hit his stride when they brought in Scottie Pippin and, under the direction of coach Phil Jackson, perfected the triangle offense, which has been called "the single most dominant offensive attack (in any major sport) of the past 20 years."[20]

It took the right players with the right coach, who saw what Jordan and his teammates were capable of and helped them form the right strategy, to create a devastatingly effective team. Indeed, Jordan, Pippen, and the Bulls, led by Phil Jackson, played what is generally considered to be the greatest season of NBA basketball in history, 1995 to 1996, when they recorded seventy-two wins and just ten losses and had both the best offensive *and* defensive rating in the NBA.

In far too many companies, employees with tremendous potential are woefully underappreciated and underutilized. They could go out and change the world if they had the right culture, the right team, and good coaching, but instead, they usually end up quitting.

We've seen people with poor performance leave a company, go down the road to another company to do roughly the same work, and suddenly they excel. They become rock stars in the new company because their real potential gets unlocked.

You may have an A-player hiding in your ranks right now, an underutilized rock star who is capable of far more than you

20   Chuck Klosterman, "What Ever Happened to the Triangle Offense?," *Grantland* (blog), January 18, 2012, http://grantland.com/features/chuck-klosterman-phil-jackson-tex-winter-death-triangle-offense/.

realize. You've never seen them truly shine because you haven't yet given them what they need to achieve their best.

We know of a company that got hijacked by ransomware and found themselves on the brink of ruin. But a worker in their warehouse just happened to have a passion for cybersecurity. He stepped up and helped the company identify the source of the ransomware, which had come from another worker clicking on a phishing email link on a company computer. The warehouse worker was able to restore the system, make it virus free, and lock it down against future attacks.

At the time, this guy was making $15 an hour, and he single-handedly saved the company. He's now making $85 an hour as their head of cybersecurity. They had a superstar there all along; they just didn't know it.

Expect the best, help people become their best, and maintain high standards, because when you have the right *people* united around the right *purpose*, give them the right *playbooks*, and encourage high *performance*, you reap tremendous *profit*.

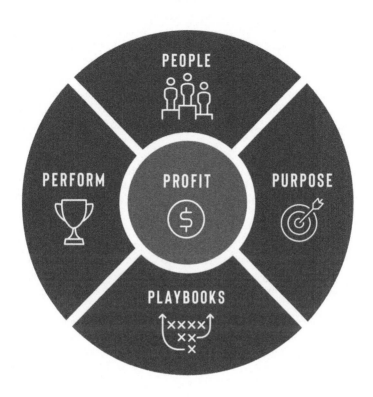

THE PERFORMANCE PRINCIPLE:
ACTIONS TO TAKE

- At the root of all performance problems, there's usually a lack of clear expectations and no scoreboard. Every single team member in your organization needs to know the score at all times.

- Give your people the numbers they need to track their own performance, and then provide the guidance they need to bring those numbers up.

- Your company's flywheel is composed of five to seven elements. First, there's your strategic differentiator. Then there are various elements that tie into your strategy. Get the flywheel moving by strengthening each of the components, and growing and scaling your business will get easier over time.

- An A-player needs great coaching, great training, *and* ongoing encouragement. Use regular coaching conversation to highlight the positive while also addressing problem areas.

PROFITS AND CASH FLOW

"Profit is what happens when you do everything else right."

—YVON CHOUINARD

If you're a small business, you're probably not making a lot of money. Cash comes in, and cash goes out, but you always seem to be on the verge of going broke. You don't necessarily realize how bad things are until one day you can't make payroll or cover your utility bills. In that way, profit is like oxygen. You don't realize how much you need it until suddenly you don't have it.

These days, companies are doing everything in their power to achieve the lowest possible cost. Banners declare, "We will not be undersold," or "Nobody sells for less," or "Expect more, pay less." Honestly, it's a terrible way to do business. If you're a construction company making 2 percent profit moving cement, the marketplace clearly doesn't place a lot of value on what you have to offer. They're not willing to pay much for it.

You might have a great company full of great people and great equipment, but if the work you do isn't valuable in the marketplace, then you're never going to grow or scale your business. On the other hand, there are some tech companies that make more than 35 percent net profit. Why are they able to charge so much for their products? Because what they do is considered much more valuable in the marketplace.

There's a reason why some attorneys make a little more than $100,000 a year and others make over a million. Why are some attorneys able to charge so much more? It's not because they're practicing under a different law. It's because their services are perceived as more valuable in the marketplace. If that construction company making 2 percent profit could convince the marketplace that they're more valuable, then people would be willing to pay more for the same services, and their net profit would increase.

PROFIT PROVIDES PROOF

Profit is proof that the marketplace values your company. But here's the thing: The marketplace pays you what *you* decide you're worth. If a lawyer says (explicitly or implicitly), "I'm worth $125 an hour," then that's what people are going to pay. If another lawyer down the street says, "I'm worth $500 an hour," then people are going to pay a lot more. And, in fact, when clients see the cost difference, they will assume the more expensive lawyer delivers better results.

In every industry, there's competition, and some companies make ten times the profit as other companies offering the same products and services. If you want to create a business that can grow and scale, you have to convince the marketplace that you're worth more. To do that, you *really* must want it!

There's a story told about Socrates that has been floating around the internet for years. It goes something like this:

In ancient Athens, a young man traveled far to seek the famous philosopher Socrates. When he finally found him, he said, "Sir, I want knowledge more than anything else in the world. Can you help me acquire it?"

Socrates replied, "Certainly, my son. Walk with me."

Socrates set off on foot and headed towards the sea, and the young man followed. Once they reached the shore, Socrates kept walking right into the water. The young man was confused, but he kept following.

Finally, when both were chest deep in the ocean, Socrates put his hands on top of the young man's head and forced him under the water. Being strong, Socrates was able to hold him there as the seconds passed, though the young man fought and struggled. Finally, after a full minute had passed, he released his hold, and the young man lunged to the surface and gasped for air. Without explanation, Socrates, turned and walked away.

The young man was shocked. He had come a long way to talk to this respected philosopher, but Socrates had tried to drown him! He ran after the old philosopher and shouted, "Sir, I asked you to help me acquire knowledge, and all you did was hold me underwater! Why?"

"Young man," Socrates said calmly, "when you were under the water, what did you want more than anything in the world?"

"I wanted to breathe," the man replied.

"Well," Socrates said, "when you want knowledge with the same intensity that you wanted to breathe, then you'll be ready to learn."

Replace the word "knowledge" with "profit," and we could say the same thing about the business world. Some leaders think their business is successful because they see big numbers in their top line (their gross revenue), but the number that really matters is the bottom line. That's your income after expenses—your profit—and it's the money that's going to fund all the great things you want to do for your company. If there's nothing in your bottom line, then you can't reinvest in your company or your people.

These days, many people, even some business leaders, treat profit like a dirty word, but without profit, you can't pay for new facilities or buy new equipment. You can't provide wage increases, generous vacation pay, or a good healthcare plan. Profit makes everything possible.

Unfortunately, most employees have been conditioned to think that profit refers to cash the owner hoards in a safe in their base-ment. That's rarely the case. Good leaders strive to be profitable not just for the money itself but because of what it means for the growth and success of their company, the better experience they can create for employees and customers.

And it's not enough to simply say, "We want to be profitable." At Pinnacle, we always recommend that people set a specific profit goal for the year. Most companies set a *revenue* goal instead, and then they cross their fingers and hope they get to the end of the year and have some profit left over. However, for all the risk and hard work, we think you should set a profit goal first.

When you have a clear purpose as an organization that every employee feels connected to, then you can start to have conversations about profit as it ties into that purpose. Suddenly, profit isn't seen as money the owner is stashing away somewhere. It's the primary resource that enables you to do bigger and better things in pursuit of your "Just Cause" and purpose. When you communicate this clearly, every team member can see why profit matters.

CHAPTER THIRTEEN

THE POWER OF ONE

A mere 1 percent improvement in some key part of your company can make all the difference in beating the competition. We call this "The Power of One," and if you can get everyone in your organization to embrace this concept, it will be revolutionary.

Imagine a 1 percent increase in your closing ratio, a 1 percent improvement in delivery speed, 1 percent fewer recordable incidents. It might not sound like much, but if you have teams throughout your organization making 1 percent improvements, the compounding effect will be astronomical.

The Power of One gives every individual and every team an easy number to work toward, a number that feels highly achievable. All you must do is get everyone in the company to make things 1 percent easier, 1 percent faster, or 1 percent more effective. Often, that's all it takes to transform your entire organization.

In NASCAR, the winner often wins a four-hundred-mile race by a fraction of a second. In a PGA golf tournament, the winner often wins by a single stroke. In the Kentucky Derby, the winning horse often crosses the finish line ahead of the next horse by mere inches. The smallest of margins can make the difference between victory and defeat. The same is true in most industries.

A COMPOUNDING EFFECT

Michael works with a restaurant company that was struggling with slim profit margins, but they were hesitant to raise their prices. Many companies feel the same way. They are afraid to raise their prices because they don't want to anger loyal customers.

As the restaurant's owner said, "When we raise prices, customers complain, and when customers complain, they don't come back."

Leaders who say this kind of thing are usually thinking of price increases in larger blocks: a 5 percent increase here, a 10 percent increase there. What if, instead, you applied the Power of One?

"What if you raised the price of every item on your menu by 1 percent?" Michael said.

The burgers ranged from $9.25 to $15.50, fries were $7.50 to $9.25, and drinks from the bar ranged from $8.50 to $12.25. Their average ticket value per guest was hovering around $28. What difference would it make if we implemented a 1 percent across-the-board price increase? Would they see a measurable drop in guest count if the average ticket went from $28.00 to $28.28?

The answer was a clear, "No, it's a change that almost no one would notice or complain about."

Michael had them look at how many guests they served across all of their locations over the course of a year, and how much more revenue that 1 percent increase would add up to. At nearly $80 million in revenue, the Power of One focus on price would generate roughly $800,000 in additional profit, without requiring the company to spend any additional cash to capture it.

Suddenly, it made sense to them, and the fear of raising prices went away.

The Power of One makes improvement achievable while simultaneously eliminating the fear of big changes. There are usually several areas in any company that would benefit from a 1 percent improvement, and when 1 percent improvements are spread throughout the organization, it has a compounding effect that can, over time, add up to a profound transformation.

Imagine the compounding effect not only of the 1 percent price increase for the burger bar, but what if the marketing team also focused on driving a 1 percent increase in traffic, the operations team focused on a 1 percent decrease in prime cost, and the finance team focused on a 1 percent increase in net cash flow? Suddenly, when you start adding up the multiple effects of a Power of One mindset, an $800,000 improvement to the bottom line, and to cash flow, is just the beginning.

CHAPTER FOURTEEN

PROFITS-FIRST DISCIPLINE

There's a formula in accounting that's been around for so long it's considered standard practice. It goes like this: **Revenue – Expenses = Profit**. In other words, you take the amount of money you bring in, subtract your expenses, and what's leftover is your profit.

This simple formula causes most organizations to constantly bet on the future because they're chasing profitability.

"Maybe if we do more, sell more, win more, we'll wind up with a bit more profit at the end of the year," they say.

But as the fiscal year goes by, the organizational costs feel like a cash-eating monster, and leaders just hope to pull out a win at the end. It's a bit like betting on a horse in the Kentucky Derby. You're hoping that somehow she'll pull ahead and get her nose over the finish line.

DON'T WAIT FOR PROFIT

Mike Michalowicz, in his book *Profit First*, recommends a very different mindset. He suggests putting profit first instead of viewing it as the money leftover at the end.[21] Think of it this way. When Greg was growing up, his father was the bread-winner. His father would come home and give his mother his paycheck for the week, and she would separate the cash out into different piles.

Then she took a few envelopes. One was marked "rent." Another was marked "groceries." A third was marked "entertainment." And so on. She would place an exact amount in each envelope, and that was the family's budget for each of those categories for the week. It ensured that every category got some funding.

Now, imagine if, instead of waiting to see if you'll have profit leftover at the end of the year, you set aside a predetermined amount of money as profit *every time you bring in money from a sale*. We usually recommend clients set aside 8 percent as a starting point (if they have less than 5 percent now), and once a month, we have them place that predetermined percentage into a separate account.

This ensures that your company is *permanently profitable*. Placing the profit in a separate account is key to making this work. If your profit is sitting in the same account as the rest of your money, you're going to wind up spending it. Set it aside—out of sight, out of mind—and it's guaranteed to be there at the end of the year. Along the way, if you need money for some expense,

---

21   Mike Michalowicz, Profit First: Transform Your Business from a Cash-Eating Monster to a Money-Making Machine (New York: Portfolio Penguin, 2017).

you raise prices or reduce operational costs—you get it from somewhere else!

THE ENTERTAINMENT ENVELOPE

When Greg was a kid, if his family used up all the money from the "entertainment" envelope, then they were done paying for entertainment that week. They didn't dip into the other envelopes. That's where discipline comes in. You don't touch the money in the profit account to cover expenses. You are paying your company first.

This tactic shouldn't sound all that strange. People do similar things all the time in their personal lives. They set aside money for a college fund, an IRA, a 401(k), or whatever else, and they don't touch it for any of their ongoing expenses. For the time being, they pretend like that money doesn't exist.

If you can do it in your personal life, surely you can implement a similar discipline in your organization. Every time money comes into your organization, set aside a fixed percentage as profit. Put that profit money into a separate account each month and wait until the end of the year to touch it.

Pay yourself first. Put a percentage of your money away *up front* and learn to live off the rest. If you set aside 8 percent as profit, then you live off the 92 percent. That's the profit-first discipline. Instead of "revenue – expenses = profit," it's "revenue – profits = expenses." And it ensures that your business is *always profitable*.

What percentage of profit should you be setting aside to put you in the top quartile of your industry? What's holding you back from being more profitable? Is it your approach to profit?

Traditional Model: Revenue – Expenses = Profit

Profit-First Model: Revenue – Profit = Expenses

CHAPTER FIFTEEN

INTERNAL FINANCIAL LITERACY

Owners of entrepreneurial organizations are often uncomfortable sharing too much financial information with their leadership teams. They're afraid that if they talk about money too much, team members will think, "All we're doing is working hard to line the boss's pockets. All leaders talk about is money, money, money!"

And so, to avoid this perception, they don't talk about money at all. As a result, most of the key stakeholders in the company are financially illiterate. The owner is the only one who knows about—and worries about—margin creep, or cash flow problems, or all the other things that owners worry about. Most people in the organization are operating blind. They really have no idea how the business is doing financially.

DARE TO OPEN THE BOOKS

Unless you share the financial data with people, they have no real idea if they're up or down, ahead or behind, so they don't know how to play the game well. If you don't share the financials, nobody actually knows how they're doing, and most of the time, they're going to assume they must be doing well.

In fact, some company owners use this to their advantage. They tell their leadership team things like, "Our labor costs are too high. Our material costs are too high. We're not making any money," but they're just gaslighting the team to get them fired up. However, since the leaders are financially illiterate, they can neither prove nor disprove the owner's claim. That's a dangerous way to operate a business.

The book *The Great Game of Business*, by Bo Burlingham and Jack Stack, recommends practicing open-book management, where you give every employee in the organization all of the information they need in order to understand how the company is doing as a whole.[22] When Jack Stack's own company, SRC Holdings in Springfield, Missouri, implemented this approach in the 1980s, it transformed the business financially.

At the time, SRC had been struggling to keep up with growing international competition in the manufacturing industry, particularly companies from Japan who were astutely learning about customer needs and adapting to meet them. Under the old system, regular employees at SRC rarely knew the financial particulars of the company. Bosses sent mixed messages

---

22 Jack Stack and Bo Burlingham, *The Great Game of Business: The Only Sensible Way to Run a Company* (New York: Crown Business, 1992).

because they didn't want to share the real numbers, but the truth was, they were taking a beating in the market.

Finally, Jack decided to do something about it. He wanted to make sure that each employee had a stake in their own future, so he began engaging them in the actual financial operation of the company. He taught them how their individual activities impacted the bottom line, and he opened up the books, so they had real numbers to work with. Now, each employee could track exactly how their hard work was contributing to the performance of the organization.

He called this "Open-Book Management," and it created an organization full of highly engaged employees at all levels. It also helped them compete in the marketplace, made them more competitive, and transformed them from a company on the brink of bankruptcy to a highly profitable company generating over $500 million in sales with about 2,000 employees.[23]

When your people can see the actual numbers and understand how their own performance ties into those numbers, it gives them a deeper stake in the well-being of the company. It teaches them financial literacy, so they are armed with the information they need to make better and more impactful decisions from day to day.

There's a financial exercise we sometimes take business leaders through. Using a photocopy of a dollar bill (no sense in damaging real money), we make a series of lines along the back, creating several segments, which we mark with things

23   "SRC," Datanyze, accessed January 30, 2023, https://www.datanyze.com/companies/src/90392190.

like "overhead 12%," "cost of goods sold 30%," "cost of labor 33%," "facilities cost 9%," "cost of reworks 8%," and so on. Then we say, "Okay, you're a $15 million company, but this is what's actually happening with every dollar we bring in."

And we proceed to cut away each section of the dollar bill. "This is going to overhead. This is going to cost of goods. This is going to labor." In the end, they have a tiny sliver of the dollar left, which we hand to them.

"This is what you are actually making from each dollar," we say.

Suddenly, the millions they're bringing in don't seem so impressive, but the real point of the exercise is to show them how financial discipline in specific areas of the company makes a tangible impact on their overall financial well-being. If individual teams understand their own financial contribution, if the numbers are "out in the open," they can become better financial stewards of their slice of that dollar bill.

The same exercise can be done with a hundred pennies. The result is the same. It's a visual exercise to show the importance of profit and align the impact of each person's performance with an understanding of what is leftover in the end. Without clear numbers, the people working on the frontlines might not realize the real monetary impact of making a mistake. People might not realize the real financial effect of operational inefficiencies. Open the books, make the actual numbers clear to people in a way that is digestible, and they can make smarter decisions in their areas of responsibility.

Conversely, if you keep your people in the dark financially, then the owner becomes the sole source of informed decision-making and bears the full weight for improving financial performance. That's a burden almost no one can handle alone.

To begin, educate and empower your leaders, then your mid-managers, and then the stakeholders who are closer to the frontlines, so they can start making informed decisions about their areas of responsibility. This will make the whole organization more intelligent and help you drive the economic engine of your business to better fulfill your purpose.

Remember, the fuel in that engine is profit and cash. When you educate your people and help them become financially literate about the business, they can begin contributing with clarity to your profits and cash flow. That, in turn, gives you more fuel in the engine and drives you to fulfill your purpose faster and on a grander scale.

DELEGATE THE BURDEN

If you will broaden the financial literacy in your business, you can start to delegate some of the burden of financial performance to other people. Michael and the leadership team in his manufacturing company came up with an effective method for doing this. Here's how it works: Take every line item on the company financial statement and, using a functional account-ability chart, assign a champion or owner for each line item.

At the end of the month, produce a report called a "Budget to Actual Variance Analysis," which can be turned into an Excel spreadsheet that is printed and distributed to the leadership team. For each line item, it will show where the company has either beat their numbers or missed them, and each of those items will have the name of a champion or owner beside it. The leadership team can then go through the spreadsheet in a monthly financial review meeting, noting any meaningful deviations from the budget. If a line item is off, the accountable person is expected to present the reason why it's off, as well as what they plan to do to get it back on track.

By sharing accountability for the company's financial performance in this way, the entire leadership team becomes far more financially literate about the company. They start asking smarter questions and connecting more with the finance team, and they gain a real understanding of what is going on in terms of actual dollars in the areas where they have the most influence.

At the time Michael implemented this tactic in his company, only two of the five people on his leadership team had completed their college educations. The rest only had high school diplomas. However, they'd gained quite a bit of experience in their careers and earned their way into leadership. Despite this lack of formal education, the process of assigning accountability for line items on the company's financial statements taught them how to ask highly intelligent questions about the company's finances.

For example, a leader might approach the Controller and say, "One of my expense lines is off. Can I get a copy of the general ledger for this account?" Then they would go through the ledger, looking for specific items that caused the mistake just so they could truly understand exactly why the number was off. Over time, Michael's leadership team developed deep financial intelligence, which led to better financial performance throughout the organization, and as a bonus, it took much of the burden off Michael.

If you get the right people on your team, give them a purpose and playbooks, and help them perform at a high level, then you're going to have a healthier and more profitable business that can pay people better, create better facilities, acquire better tools, and do more. It's as simple as that. We've simplified that to a formula:

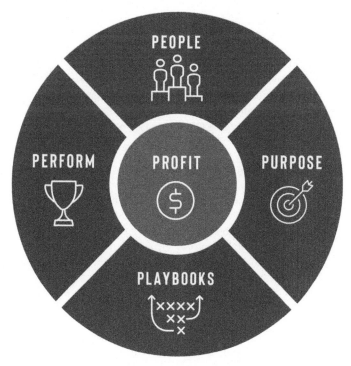

People + Purpose + Playbooks + Perform = Profit

Of course, every company wants to be successful, but you can't get rich by demanding it. Companies that are profitable generally hire great people and take care of them. They communicate a clear purpose throughout their organization and create well-documented playbooks to train people on all of their processes. They encourage high performance in a variety of ways, and the output of all these principles is profit—profit that can be used to grow and scale the business to achieve more than you dared to dream!

THE PROFIT PRINCIPLE: ACTIONS TO TAKE

- Profit is proof that the marketplace values your company. If you want to create a business that can grow and scale, then you have to convince the marketplace that you're worth more.

- Profit makes everything possible. It's not a dirty word. It's the primary resource that enables you to do bigger and better things in pursuit of your "Just Cause" and purpose. When you communicate this clearly, every team member can see why profit matters.

- Often, all it takes to transform your entire organization is to get everyone in the company to make things 1 percent easier, 1 percent faster, or 1 percent more effective.

- Instead of waiting to see if you'll have profit leftover at the end of the year, set aside a predetermined amount of money as profit every time you bring in money from a sale. This ensures that your company is permanently profitable.

- Broaden the financial literacy in your business so you can delegate some of the burden to other people. Take every line item on the company financial statement and assign a champion or owner for each line item.

CONCLUSION

Experience plays a pivotal role in the business landscape. The past five decades have witnessed a revolution in business practices driven by technology, and the rapid advancement of artificial intelligence promises to further accelerate this transformation. Amidst these momentous shifts, the foundational principles of Pinnacle have remained steadfastly relevant, holding true today as they would have half a century ago.

At the heart of Pinnacle lies the convergence of two crucial components:

1. A flexible approach to Business Operating Systems that seamlessly adapts and evolves alongside a company's growth trajectory. This adaptability ensures that our solutions remain effective and applicable in the face of the ever-changing business landscape.
2. Accomplished and knowledgeable guides with extensive experience. These guides possess the expertise to skillfully tailor the tools and strategies to address the unique and spe-

cific needs of each client. Through their guidance, we create a customized and personalized experience that maximizes the potential for success.

By combining these elements, Pinnacle offers a comprehensive and holistic package that empowers businesses to thrive in the dynamic and competitive modern business world.

Should the concepts and stories about our distinctive approach resonate with you, we encourage you not to settle for a "one-size-fits-all" approach to growing your business. We firmly believe in the necessity of building your own personalized and customized Business Operating System, tailored specifically to your unique business requirements. As you strive to grow and evolve, your approach must also adapt and evolve accordingly. This is why, at Pinnacle, we advocate for an approach to Business Operating Systems that can change and adjust to meet your current needs. While a rigid or restrictive system may provide temporary value, it can eventually hinder your progress. In contrast, our approach can flexibly accommodate your evolving needs.

Every business operates within a system that is perfectly designed to yield the results it currently achieves. By studying the outputs of your business, we can assess the effectiveness of your existing system. The same principle applies to various areas of life. For instance, if you find yourself in a failing third marriage, it indicates that your system for maintaining a successful marriage is not working for you. Similarly, if your fitness routine fails to yield desired results despite your efforts, it indicates that your fitness system requires adjustment.

Perhaps you have already experimented with a Business Operating System, or perhaps you are currently using one. If you are dissatisfied with the results, experiencing limited growth, or not progressing as quickly as you should, it is possible that the system itself is the underlying issue. If the system cannot be customized to guide you toward your desired destination, it may be time to upgrade from a rigid "system" to a more adaptable "approach" that can meet you where you are and facilitate your journey to success.

TAKE THE FIRST STEP

Now that you have a thorough understanding of an alternative approach, the decision lies in your hands. This is not merely a decision to purchase something; it is a decision to embrace change. By doing so, you can position yourself as a category of one, envied in your industry, with clients and employees proud to be associated with your company. Furthermore, you have the opportunity to accelerate the growth of your business beyond what you thought possible. To surround yourself with exceptional A-players and leaders who continuously improve quarter after quarter. To foster a high-performance culture where morale is high, customers become advocates, and employee turnover is minimal. To become the preferred brand that customers choose to do business with, and employees aspire to work for.

If you're ready to embark on this transformative journey, all you need to do is commit to change and build a bigger, bolder future for your company. The path ahead may present challenges, but the view from the pinnacle of your industry will be both spectacular and immensely rewarding.

To truly become a category of one, you must create something exceptional—something scalable that grows in tandem with your business. Your vision of becoming a category-of-one company should be shared with every one of your employees and ideal customers.

To become a category of one, you need to build something special, something that provides consistent, differentiated value in the marketplace. Something that everyone believes in and can see how their individual role connects to a greater purpose. Something that makes you want to kick off the covers every morning and get right back into the game of building your business.

While you are doing that, know that our Pinnacle Business Guides are out there today working with thousands of leadership teams to help them get to their next summit. They are also searching for, and creating, the best of the best tools to add to our climbing toolbox, so the next time we are with a leadership team, it will always be better than the last time.

You can do this. Here's the simple formula to drive the point home one final time:

1. Get the right people, who believe what you believe, in the right seats.
2. Give them a crystal-clear vision and strategy (i.e., purpose) of where you are going, why it's important, and how you will get there.
3. Then capture the magic with playbooks that are simple and scalable. Remember, "complexity kills growth."

4. Coach, mentor, motivate, and encourage your team to consistently perform at a high level.

5. The profits will give you the war chest to hire A-players and provide them with a great working environment. It will also allow you to create outstanding training opportunities for your team. You can build a financial safety net so the next time you hit a recession, pandemic, or even uncover an opportunity to have someone join the team, or acquire a business, you are prepared to act.

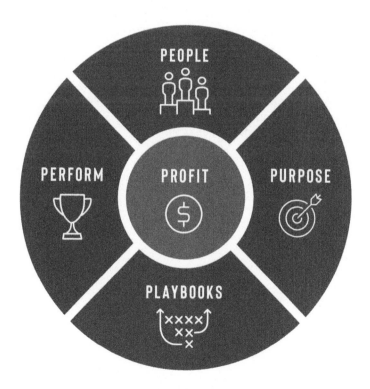

You can start right now by looking at your people, purpose, playbooks, performance, and profitability, and ask yourself, "Can we do better?"

Gregory, Michael, and our community of Certified Pinnacle Business Guides encourage you to set your sights on your pinnacle and get started on the journey using our trail map and tools.

Let's climb to the Pinnacle of Business Operating Systems!

—GREGORY CLEARY AND MICHAEL ERATH

For additional resources, further help, or to contact us directly, visit the Pinnacle Business Guides website at www.PinnacleBusinessGuides.com.

ACKNOWLEDGMENTS

From Greg: I would not be able to do this work if not for the support of my amazing soulmate and bride of thirty years, Julie. Julie has stood by my side every step of the way. Also my daughter Samantha, who teaches me more about emotional intelligence than any book. My son Benjamin, you are an inspiration. As I watch you pursue your dreams, I admire your laser focus. My family is the fuel that inspires me to kick off the covers and go be a better father, husband, and business coach every single day.

Duane Marshall, my partner in Pinnacle, and our leadership team, who do what it takes to help us build a Category of ONE Community for our guides and clients.

From Michael: I would like to first and foremost thank my lifelong friend, incredible partner, and wife, Elizabeth. It was her encouragement to transition from a twenty-year journey growing my own businesses to a brave new career of helping entrepreneurs grow hundreds of businesses. The lives we are able to impact has grown exponentially, and I could not have made the pivot without her encouragement and endless support. I would also like to thank Cameron Herold as well as my former YPO and EO forummates for helping me grow and always challenging me to push myself further than I would have on my own.

From both of us: The inspiration behind this book is the work we get to do with our clients. We have a front row seat with visionaries who are creating "Category of ONE Companies" in virtually every industry. We see the impact of the tools we teach, the decisions we help the leadership teams make, the results of those decisions, and how they lead to record-setting performance. We also see and learn significant lessons from the companies that struggle and the teams that don't perform. Getting to see what works and what doesn't with such clarity has compelled us to share our insights with the world.

We would not be here without the amazing guides we have had the opportunity to work with during our time in EOS, Scaling Up, and now Pinnacle Business Guides and Michael's Phoenix-based firm, Next Level Growth.

To all of the Guides who help build the tools, teach each other, and do amazing work every day with clients. You help us prove that these tools and concepts work. Thank you for your commitment to be the very best at our craft.

We are also very thankful to the thousands of clients who have partnered with us and our community of guides over the years to do this work and are committed to holding us accountable, giving us feedback on the work we do, and then opening the door to refer us to their friends and peers.

Finally, we are thankful to you, the reader. Visionaries and leadership team members of small- to mid-market companies are the ones who are creating most of the innovation; new ideas; new job openings; and strong, healthy cultures where people love to come to work and enjoy the people they work with. Thank you for working to be a better leader this year than you were last year. We hope you incorporate these ideas into your organization as well as your own personal growth plan.

"Every mountaintop is within reach if you just keep climbing!"

—GREGORY AND MICHAEL

ABOUT THE AUTHORS

Gregory Cleary is the founder of Pinnacle Business Guides, a former certified Scaling Up coach, author of *Pinnacle: Five Principles That Take Your Business to the Top of the Mountain* with Steve Preda, and a former certified EOS implementer. Greg wants to disrupt the Business Operating System industry by helping clients reach the pinnacle of their industry with a personalized Business Operating System. Pinnacle is obsessed with curating the finest tools to help visionary entrepreneurs build businesses. You can reach Greg at www.PinnacleBusinessGuides.com.

Michael spent the first twenty years of his career growing his family's manufacturing business to $45 million with over 200 employees before becoming the first Pinnacle Business Guide behind founders Greg Cleary and Duane Marshall. Michael is the founder of Next Level Growth and, in 2017, published his first best-seller, *RISE: The Reincarnation of an Entrepreneur*. You can reach Michael at www.NextLevelGrowth.com.

Made in the USA
Monee, IL
15 July 2023

39039664R00111